# MEET ME AT...
## THE GARDEN...
## DETOUR...CROSS
### A SPIRITUAL SMORGASBORD
### WITH AN OCCASIONAL BURP OF HUMOR

# JOANNE WILLIAMS

for Pat,
Blessings
Joanne Williams

outskirtspress
DENVER, COLORADO

Outskirts Press, Inc.
http://www.outskirtspress.com

ISBN:  978-1-4787-1603-7

Outskirts Press and the "OP" logo are trademarks belonging to Outskirts Press, Inc.

PRINTED IN THE UNITED STATES OF AMERICA

# Contents

# Acknowledgements

THIS BOOK IS dedicated to my children: Diane, Julie, Cindy and Dave. It was Dave who suggested I put these messages into print. I presented them at a variety of protestant churches in southeast Idaho over a number of years. Dave reminded me that none of the children were present to hear them because we live so far apart.

Roger Kottke was the most thorough editor I have worked with. Thanks, Rog, for your patience, skill and expertise.

Biblical references are from THE LIVING BIBLE and THE NEW INTERNATIONAL VERSION.

All the contemporary stories are real. Some names have been changed.

# Daffodils

I WANT TO tell you about an email I received. It seems the writer, Emma, lives in Laguna, California by the ocean and her adult daughter, Carolyn, lives at Arrowhead, in the mountains. Carolyn called her mother and said, "You must come and see the daffodils before they are over." Emma wasn't crazy about the two hour drive but she reluctantly agreed to go the following Tuesday. The weather was miserable and, as she drove up the mountain, the road was almost invisible from clouds and fog. Upon arrival, she said, "Forget the daffodils. I'm not budging out of this house until I leave to go home. Besides, I'm perfectly happy just to be here with my grandchildren." Carolyn insisted and said she was used to driving in that weather so they packed up the children and set out. After about 20 minutes, they turned onto a gravel road where there was a small church and on the far side of the church was a hand lettered sign with an arrow that read "Daffodil Garden."

"We each took a child's hand," Emma wrote, "and I followed Carolyn down the path. Then, as we turned a corner, I looked up and gasped. Before me lay the most glorious sight. It looked as though someone had taken a great vat of gold and poured it over the mountain peak and its surrounding slopes. Different colored varieties were planted in large groups so that it swirled and flowed like its own river with its own unique hue.

e five acres of flowers."

did this?" Emma asked. Carolyn replied, "Just one woman. She lives on the property in that home" and she pointed to a modest A-frame in the midst of all the glory. We walked up to the house. On the patio was a poster that said, "Answer to questions you may be asking." The first answer was, "50,000 bulbs." The second answer was, "One at a time, by one woman; two hands, two feet and one brain." The third answer was, "Began in 1958." The writer added, "It was a life-changing experience that I, one bulb at a time, could so dramatically change the world around me.

As you symbolically look at the garden of experiences *you* have created, what do you see; flowers and shrubs and things of beauty or are you staring at parched ground where nothing but weeds and thorns will grow? Sometimes, we become so engrossed with the decay around us that there is no room in our garden for much good. The ground is parched. When we think kindly of others we add beauty to their garden but our own garden is also blessed. Not only that, the beauty in our garden multiplies! Have you ever planted daffodils? What happens? The next year, where you planted five bulbs, many more are there. Sometimes, they are so anxious to thrill you; they pop up through the last snow. I'm not quite sure how that works.

There will always be people in our lives who seem to enjoy being mean and ugly. They thrive on making others miserable and, sometimes, we cannot avoid them because we work with them or have to spend time with them. Their gardens will never show beauty or bring joy to others. If you cannot get away and cannot avoid these people, then the Bible advises in *Romans 12:17-18,* **Do not repay anyone evil for evil. Be careful to do what is right in the eyes of everybody. If it is possible, <u>as far as it depends on you,</u> live at peace with everyone.**

A bouquet from the florist is always a welcomed gift but the symbolic flowers we plant in each other's garden, with the simplest of gestures, can also be unforgettable. When my husband was terminally ill, housework sunk to low on my priority list. One day, I passed through the dining room and noticed the words, "I love you," written *in the dust* on the hutch. A flower took root in my garden and a warm spot was created in my heart.

If you want to plant a garden of beauty around you, but the people you are with want you to stand in a wasteland of weeds and thorns with them, it might be time for a change. It's hard to break away from old habits or old friends, even when they have no intention of remaining loyal. It's easier to hang on to something we know is hurting us, but that we feel we have some control over, than venture into something we know will be better but requires us to change. Here's where Jesus tells us He will help. *Romans 8: 31 & 38-39,* **If God is for us, who can be against us? For I am convinced that neither death nor life, neither angels nor demons, neither the present nor the future, nor any powers, neither height nor depth, nor anything else in all creation, will be able to separate us from the love of God that is in Christ Jesus our lord.**

When that lady planted her first daffodil, I doubt that she said to herself, "Here's how I am going to serve mankind. I will plant a bunch of flowers." She might have said to herself, "What should I do with five acres? I guess I will start over in this corner and plant a flower and see what happens. Maybe I'll plant another one." She probably had no intention to eventually serve her community and bring people from long distances to be thrilled and awe struck and even *blessed by* her efforts.

It is easy for us to just exist in the little world of our own mind and think about ourselves and how life isn't fair while God is saying, "Look at you! I created you! But I didn't make you for *you*. I made you for *Me* and I want you to get out of yourself and reflect *Me* to others by the way you live." Express that wonderful freedom by blessing others around you with a smile or a word of encouragement. If you are too shy for that, then plant a flower. The daffodil lady didn't achieve her goal overnight but she didn't stop planting until her garden was complete.

# Past

WE ALL HAVE one. It has no shape, color or sound but it has tremendous influence over us. We all have a past and much of the way we live and think today is influenced by our past. Were we well fed or hungry, clothed or in rags, abused physically or sexually or psychologically? Did we live in our natural parents' home, foster home, adoptive home, orphanage, or were we homeless? Some people seem to have escaped the hurts and disappointments of childhood but the majority of us have had our share and shaking off those memories is difficult. We carry the past around like a heavy bag of garbage that smells stronger every day.

What makes us hang on to the past? Fear? Are we afraid of people today because someone in our past caused us to be afraid? The Bible encourages us not to be afraid of others. *Psalm 27:1,* **The Lord is my light and my salvation – whom shall I fear? The Lord is the stronghold of my life; of whom shall I be afraid?** *Psalm 56:4,* **In God I trust; I will not be afraid.** Perhaps we hang on to old garbage because we enjoy the feeling of revenge, hatred or getting even. This is what the Bible says about revenge in *Romans 12:19,* **"Vengeance is <u>mine</u> says the Lord. I will repay."**

For over forty years, I attended a large Presbyterian church in a city outside of Sacramento, California. We had two services on Sunday mornings and, if you attended the 9:30 service, chances were you didn't know a lot of people who attended at 11:00 unless you saw them at coffee hour between services. I was in the choir and one Sunday a lady I recognized but didn't know well came into the choir room between services and said she needed to speak to me. We stepped away from others and into a corner for privacy. I couldn't imagine what she wanted to say. She looked at me seriously and said, "I want you to know that I have hated you for 20 years." I was stunned. I didn't hate anybody and I didn't dream that someone hated me, and for 20 years! "Before you go any farther," I said, "I want to ask your forgiveness. Obviously, I have done something serious for you to hate me for so long and I am genuinely sorry. Please tell me what caused these feelings."

She reminded me that, 20 years earlier, we had been in a first aid class together at a local community college and, although we did not even know each other's name, we recognized each other from church so, when the instructor told the class to pair off, we teamed up and were scheduled to be together for the duration of a five week course. She missed the next two sessions and, when she returned, I had a different partner and she considered that as my snubbing and abandoning her. What really happened was that, when she did not show up for the second and third classes, the teacher assigned me a different partner. I didn't give it a second thought but she chewed on it for the next 20 years. Near the end of those years, her husband became terminally ill with cancer and was served by the hospice I worked for. This association changed her opinion of me. "I watched you and the others work with my husband and saw your compassion and I could no longer harbor bad feelings toward you," she said. I thought to myself how miserable she must have been over this incident and how long her bitterness lasted without my even knowing about it.

Perhaps we hang onto the heavy, smelly load because we refuse to forgive. We say, "I will never forgive that person for what he/she did or said or implied. My life will never be the same because of that person." We seem to forget what we have done against God and yet we want judgment for others and mercy for ourselves. The Bible tells us that, if we want forgiveness, we must forgive. *Matthew: 6:14-15,* **For if you forgive men when they sin against you, your heavenly Father will also forgive you. But if you do not forgive men their sins, your Father will not forgive your sins.** *Luke: 6:37,* **Do not judge and you will not be judged. Do not condemn and you will not be condemned. Forgive and you will be forgiven.**

Sometimes our grief is so intense, our hatred so deep that we do not know who to blame so we blame God. Why not? How can a loving, compassionate God allow such sadness, such pain, to happen to innocent people? To children? I do not know the answer.

Over a period of about 15 years, I had many foster children share my home and none of them deserved the treatment they had experienced. One little girl was five years old. When I undressed her on the first night, I noticed round scar-like marks all over her little chest and back. I asked the pediatrician what they were and he said they were cigarette burns. She was so traumatized, she could not speak.

I cried out to God, "Why? Why do you allow this to happen?" Some people say that bad happens because we are born into a sinful world, and my response is, "Then, punish the sinners, not the innocent; not the children." Authors have written books about why bad things happen to good people and I still haven't read an answer that satisfies me but, this I know; through every difficulty in my life, whether I was there to help someone else or I was the victim, I felt God's presence. I could not explain or justify someone else's misbehavior, whether it was to an innocent little foster child or directed toward me, but I believed that God had a plan, even if I did not understand it.

A well worn saying is, "Forgive and forget." Another well worn saying is, "Easier said than done." I once heard a minister remark that it is possible to forgive but only God can forget and I tend to agree with him. Many of us have had unpleasant past experiences that come forward from out of nowhere in our mind and we are reliving the experience without even closing our eyes. I was fortunate enough, as an adult, to receive some helpful counseling that showed me how to forgive. I learned to forgive someone who was dead but who created memories that haunted me. I learned how to finally abandon the baggage and move ahead into freedom and peace. Bad experiences no longer have power over me.

In the Old Testament, we read about influential leaders who misused their authority in order to fill their sinful desires. King David wanted another man's wife so he had her husband put into the front line of battle and killed. David was arrogant, lustful and greedy. Then, he turned to God in repentance and received forgiveness, even for murder. David went on to serve God in powerful ways that affect us even today. He wrote the beautiful Psalms that most of us are familiar with.

In the New Testament, Saul was a hateful, vengeful, powerful person who was greatly feared because he persecuted and executed Christians. He was present at the stoning death of Steven. Then, the power of God met him on the road to Damascus and blinded him. He obediently followed God's command, accepted Him as Lord of his life, and eventually became one of the most effective evangelists of all time. God changed his name from Saul to Paul and this is the Paul we read about, the Paul who wrote much of the New Testament.

Both of these men, who lived centuries apart, had a past that was filled with arrogance and greed. They wanted things their way, even if it meant killing another person. They were confronted by a God who loved them despite their wicked ways and changed them to great men of Biblical history because they recognized their need for God's love and mercy. Each man had a wicked past but they turned away from it and did not let it influence their future.

Perhaps your past haunts you because you made some serious mistakes that cost you a high price: a job or a marriage or prison time. You feel bound up because you have regrets. We all have regrets, regardless of the reason. We all wish we had said or done something differently because the outcome would have been better. We all have the "if only" syndrome. If only I had thought before I spoke. If only I had listened better. We cannot say that destructive behavior doesn't happen to us. It happens. We don't love the destructive habit or the addiction or behavior, but God is telling us to use them as stepping stones and not stumbling blocks. *Do not get so hung up on the past that you cannot see the possibilities for the future.* You're alive. You're here and God has a plan for you that will give you satisfaction with your life and peace with Him.

We have a choice. We can say, "No, I'm sorry but I like being bitter and making those around me uncomfortable and bitter, too. I like the frown in my brow that shows the world I am unhappy. I like being depressed and not sleeping and wondering if I will ever be happy again I like the stomach ache that comes from worry and the attention I get when I complain; negative attention but attention, nevertheless. Just one more reminder to others of how miserable I am."

Or, we can say, "I'm tired of being tired. I recognize that

my bitterness only hurts me and, as I drag this garbage of hurt and anger, it pulls me down and wears me out. Worst of all, it does me harm. I'm tired of my attitude. Actually, it surprises me that anyone even wants my company. The ones who love me seem to put up with me but I know they wish I felt better. It's time, Lord. It's time to listen to you, to accept your invitation to be free of past hurts. It's time to forgive those people who have hurt me so deeply -- and let go of the anger. I'm willing to take that big leap and then I can come to you, Lord, and ask you to forgive me for what I have become as a result of hanging on to the past.

Help me, Lord. Change me now that I am free of the old baggage that took so much of my time and energy. Use me, Lord, to reflect your love." *Jeremiah 29:11:* **For I know the plans I have for you, declares the Lord, plans to prosper you and not to harm you, plans to give you hope and a future.**

# A Personal Christmas

ONE OF THE most beautiful stories in the Bible is the Christmas Story. Christmas cards depict Joseph leading the donkey with Mary riding on their way to Bethlehem. They show the manger scene or shepherds looking up at the bright star or wise men bearing gifts for the newborn king. It was an event that changed the people there and then the world.

In some versions of the Bible, Mary is described as being "great with child." Could that have influenced the innkeeper? He probably sensed by just looking at her that she was close to delivery and ushered them to the stable.

Our family once had an innkeeper take pity on us when there was no room and arranged for a most unusual accommodation. My husband and I took our young daughters on a camping trip through the northwest and into Canada. We had a pickup truck and small camper that the four of us squeezed uncomfortably into at night. We took a ferry to Victoria on Vancouver Island and, as we neared land, the Empress Hotel caught our eye and the children, not yet teen agers, were especially excited because it resembled a castle.

My husband sensed their awe and announced, "We have spent every night cramped in the little camper. Tonight, we shall sleep in a castle." He confidently opened the oversized door into the Empress Hotel and we entered the magnificent lobby.

At the reservation desk, my husband requested a room with a view and was told there was nothing available. He lowered his standards a bit and was given the same answer. Disappointed, he mentioned to the desk clerk that our children had looked forward to staying in a castle just one night. The innkeeper apparently took pity on the children and said there was a room they didn't ordinarily rent out. It was used by Staff but was vacant that night. We followed his directions, took the elevator as far up as it would go, found an unmarked metal door, opened it and climbed many steep steps to a small room. The window was open and birds flew in and out. It was quite perfect for our purpose and it had a view of the water. An innkeeper took pity on us and, although the accommodation was far from what we had hoped, it filled our need perfectly. The experience made wonderful memories.

The manger scene was also not what Joseph hoped for to welcome the special child but it was the best available and the couple settled in and waited.

Shepherds were humble folk, resigned to doing the same job for the rest of their lives. Uneducated and poor, they handled routine well. It was the unexpected that flustered them and the Bible says they were terrified when the angel appeared, the light shown, the angel spoke and a heavenly host praised God. Why shouldn't they be terrified! Something very frightening was happening and they may have feared for their lives until the angel calmed them and announced the good news of Jesus' birth.

The angel told the shepherds where Jesus was and how to identify Him and off they went to see this event that had come to pass. And then, they spread the word of what had happened, what the angel said, and people who heard were amazed. The shepherds, the simplest of people, were suddenly bearers of good news of great joy. They would never be the same. In their old age, they would pass down the account of their meeting with the angel to generations that followed. They had witnessed the Christ child. This event in Bethlehem caused them to change from a quiet group of lower-class citizens to bold and excited evangelists. *Luke 2:17,* **they spread the word concerning what had been told them about this child, and all who heard it were amazed at what the shepherds said to them.**

Directly opposite of the shepherds were the Magi, wise men, possibly scientists or astronomers. The Bible says they came from the East and were led to the Christ child by a star. We do not know how long it took them to travel. It may have been a year. According to the Bible, they came to the *house,* bowed down and worshiped the child and brought precious gifts of gold, incense and myrrh.

While on their journey they were directed by King Herod in Jerusalem to find the child and report back to him so he could also go and worship him. King Herod's real purpose was to kill the young Jesus because he feared the prophesy of this child who was reported to become king of the Jews according to scripture. The Wise Men sabotaged King Herod's evil plan by not obeying his orders but, instead, returned to their homeland by way of another route. They had been warned in a dream not to go back to Herod. Something they had no way of foreseeing interrupted their journey and they had to change their course. *Matt. 2: 12,* **Then, being divinely warned in a dream that they should not return to Herod, they departed for their own country another way.**

As we think of the Christmas story, where do you and I fit into this picture? How do we relate to Jesus today? Are we like the innkeeper, basking in the success of our comfortable life with no need to accommodate Him? Are we willing to give Him only the "stable" of our life because we don't want our routine disrupted? Are we like the shepherds - stuck in a boring job, never any extra money, little social life outside of a few people who are also stuck in boring jobs? Are we terrified at the thought of God speaking to *us*, directing *us* through friends or strangers to explore a faith that includes Him? Though frightened, the shepherds were curious enough to listen and obey the directions of the angel. They found the Christ child and immediately told others about their experience. No longer were they nobody. They were now instruments of hope, echoes of prophecy. They seized the opportunity to spread joy. Plain, ordinary, uneducated, unsophisticated, naïve; these shepherds would never be the same. They had an energy that propelled them through the hum drum of routine to a hope that stretched into the future, far beyond just their work. They had a story to tell.

You have a story to tell. Life is boring and routine sometimes but it also has exciting moments and great experiences. You will be directed just as surely as the shepherds were if you are willing to listen.

Are we like the Magi, looking for Christ on an intellectual level? Nothing wrong with that. They had a desire, a drive to find Him and worship Him and bring Him gifts. They must have been fascinated by the unusual star that led them but, whatever the reason; they humbled themselves before the Christ child and brought gifts that acknowledged Him as a future king. If your plans or goals become something other than what you intended, look to God for a change in direction. The Magi carefully set out to follow a prescribed plan and then something happened that they knew nothing about nor could they change. They were given instruction in a dream they could have ignored but, instead, obeyed and returned home a different way. Perhaps you had the best intentions when you set your goals but circumstances, over which you had no control, now suggest you try a new direction. If the Magi had not changed their plans, Jesus may have been murdered. The Magi didn't know this when they followed God's leading.

If good intentions led you to disappointment you could neither foresee nor change, take your leading from the Magi. They returned home via a different route; possibly one that was longer or more difficult but it led safely to their final destination. Trust God's perfect leading.

# Mary's World

PROBABLY IN HER early teens, she had committed an unpardonable sin by becoming pregnant prior to marriage. The Bible tells us that she was betrothed to a man, a binding agreement much more serious and difficult to get out of than breaking an engagement today. If she was found to have had sexual relations with another man during this betrothal, it was legal for the men of the town to stone her to death. Her fiancé sincerely loved her and wanted to protect her so he decided to divorce her from the engagement in order to save her from public disgrace. We can only imagine what was going on in *his* mind. "Who could she have been with? Why did she do this? Why would she bring disgrace to me?" Then he had a dream where an angel of the Lord appeared and revealed that all this was the Lord's plan, prophesied hundreds of years earlier by Isaiah. The angel advised him to take his fiancée into his home as his wife. And so, Joseph awoke and obeyed the command of the angel and took Mary home as his wife and had no sexual relations with her until she delivered her son and Joseph, again in obedience to the angel, gave the baby the name of Jesus.

Every mother has her own secret hopes and dreams for her baby. She prays that it will be strong and healthy with eyes that see well and ears that hear well. She daydreams of the baby growing to be a healthy child and then adult and she hopes that the child will become an honest, kind, intelligent person. As Christians, we mothers want, probably more than anything else, for our children to know the Lord and be comfortable sharing that good news through their words and behavior.

I wonder how Mary felt about her new son. I wonder what she thought through those months of pregnancy when she carried a child who had been promised to her by God. I wonder if she told anyone in the neighborhood what really happened; that the angel, Gabriel, came to her and said she was favored by God and would bear a son to become savior of the world. My guess is that she did not share this good news with the neighborhood. The angel told Mary that her cousin, Elizabeth, was also expecting a child in her old age and the Bible simply says that, upon hearing that good news, Mary hurried to Elizabeth's home in the hill country of Judea and stayed there for three months. Then, the Bible tells us of the journey to Bethlehem where Joseph registered for the census since he was from the lineage of David.

These were extremely unusual circumstances but we do know that Mary and Joseph eventually returned to Nazareth in Galilee and remained there to raise their family.

Mary knew that Jesus was a special person. The Bible tells us in Luke 2:40, **he grew and became strong, filled with wisdom and the grace of God was upon him.** Then, after a pilgrimage to Jerusalem, Mary experienced that horrible event we all fear when our child disappears. Where could he be? She and Joseph left the temple to return home and assumed that their son was somewhere in their group until they had traveled an entire day before realizing he was missing. He was twelve years old. They returned to Jerusalem and, three days later, found him

If this happened to any of us, can you just hear the reaction? *"Where in the world were you? Why didn't you let us know*

MEET ME AT…THE GARDEN…DETOUR…CROSS

*what you were doing? You know these are dangerous times with bad guys out there who could hurt you. We were ready to have an Amber Alert started. You paralyzed us with fear."* Jesus had good reason to remain behind but they did not understand. This is how Luke explains it in *Luke 2:41-51:* **Every year his parents went to Jerusalem for the Feast of the Passover. When he was twelve years old, they went up to the Feast, according to the custom. After the Feast was over, while his parents were returning home, the boy Jesus stayed behind in Jerusalem but they were unaware of it. Thinking he was in their company, they traveled on for a day. Then they began looking for him among their relatives and friends. When they did not find him, they went back to Jerusalem to look for him. After three days they found him in the temple courts, sitting among the teachers, listening to them and asking them questions. Everyone who heard him was amazed at his understanding and his answers. When his parents saw him, they were astonished. His mother said to him, "Son, why have you treated us like this? Your father and I have been anxiously searching for you." "Why were you searching for me?" he asked. "Didn't you know I had to be in my Father's house?" But they did not understand what he was saying to them. Then he went down to Nazareth with them and was obedient to them. But his mother treasured all these things in her heart. And Jesus grew in wisdom and stature and in favor with God and men.**

Have you ever had a twelve year old, or older, do something or go somewhere that was not within your plan for them and they felt perfectly comfortable about it and you did not agree or understand? You are in good company. We need to be aware that accounts in the Bible have relevance today. The Bible is truly a *living* book.

As mothers and fathers, we are fascinated by a newborn and

feel great pride and joy that this precious child has been loaned to us for a while. We have hopes and dreams that include good health, good friends, education, eventual families of their own, and a long productive life. In reality, we know the road won't always be a smooth one but, most of the time, we never dreamed it would be so full of bumps and pot holes and detours.

There are illnesses and accidents that sometimes require a long, painful, financially draining recovery. There are drugs and habits that interfere with plans and send our child in a new direction. There are some friendships and relationships that we approve of and others that we are strongly opposed to and can't do much about but we continue to have faith in our children and want good things to happen to them. We don't want them to be misunderstood. We don't want them harmed. Those things were not in our plans when we waited for our baby to be born and when we first gazed into those eyes. Sometimes our plans go rather smoothly and other times they are different from the moment of birth.

I wonder what Mary thought when her precious son left home and began preaching in the synagogue; when He made priests angry by usurping their power, healing the sick, the blind and the deaf. Then He convinced some He was the Messiah they had waited for. What did Mary think when He raised Lazarus from the dead, or later when many people turned on Him? It must have hurt her deeply to see Him ridiculed and plotted against. And then, when He was beaten and scourged and crowned with thorns that bit into his flesh and caused his precious blood to roll down his face, I wonder if she cried out inside, "No! Please no! This isn't at all what I thought would happen. I was told He would reign over the house of Jacob forever and his kingdom would never end. You don't understand. Bad people are poisoning your mind and telling you falsehoods. He is not guilty of the things you have been told. You are being misled. You are murdering the savior of the world. You are killing our Messiah. You are killing my son, my special son."

We need to remember how much Jesus loved his mother. Even in His darkest hour, as He hung painfully from the cross until He died, Jesus saw to it that his mother was going to be cared for when He was gone. He didn't look around for the disciples, to give them last minute instructions. He looked at his beloved Mother and His beloved follower, John, and told them, from then on, to think of and treat each other as mother and son. Jesus made sure His mother would be cared for by someone He loved and trusted. All this while He was dying on the cross.

We know now what the plan was because we have the Bible. We have history relayed in print. We can see the full picture and see where we fit into the picture. The Bible is a book of wisdom, parable, prophecy and just plain good down home common sense. Mary was a very special woman of God for she was chosen from all the women of all time to bear God's son. I believe she shared the same feelings for her children as other mothers throughout the ages. We can hope and dream and cry and pray, as she must have done. We can trust God, that He has a plan we might not always recognize or understand but we believe is a perfect plan, as she must have done.

Like many other people of the Bible, Mary is a shining example for us to follow. Without expecting any unusual attention or treatment from God, she trusted herself to Him. When God chose her for a special experience that required enormous faith on her part, she agreed willingly even though that experience culminated in great sadness and grief. She never faltered but pondered these things in her heart and continued to trust the

Lord. Finally, she and the rest of the world understood the reason for her special son's birth, life and death when He rose from the grave and revealed Himself as our Messiah. Whatever your experiences or hardships, know that your continued faith will lead you to eventual victory.

# Grace

GRACE, ACCORDING TO the dictionary, is a noun that denotes action. It means unexpected or undeserved love. Grace can be in the most important experience of your life; being saved from serious injury by a seat belt or carried from a burning building. Grace can also be part of the everyday nitty-gritty. Not a day passes without each one of us being touched by it; the fabric from which the lives of ordinary people, you and me, is woven. It comes in the form of a big unexpected gift or a small unexpected kiss.

When I was twenty-seven years old, my voice became husky and I had difficulty speaking and singing. A trip to the doctor revealed polyps on both of my vocal cords. The polyps were surgically removed and that was the beginning of life-changing events for me and ultimately for my family.

For the first several weeks, I was not allowed to speak at all in order to facilitate healing. Our only child at the time was 2 ½ years old and, since she couldn't read or write, I couldn't communicate with her by using a pad and pencil so we had to leave her with a friend during the daytime while my husband was at work. When the time came for me to begin talking again, special therapy taught me to speak differently, putting pressure on a part of my vocal cords that had not been used as much before. It was time consuming, exhausting and embarrassing because

I did exercises in front of a mirror and they were not pretty to watch. It was discouraging because progress was slow. When I finally regained my voice, I was cautioned not to whisper or talk on the telephone because these two activities used a lot of energy in pushing the sound.

At the time, I didn't see much grace in any of this experience but it was there in the form of a capable surgeon, a generous friend who cared for my daughter and a helpful husband. Neighbors and friends tried to make my recovery comfortable but it was hard for them to be around me because, when they talked, I couldn't answer. There was no conversation back and forth. People, even medical staff, came to within inches of my nose and spoke slowly with a louder than usual voice, as if I could not see or hear or think when all I couldn't do was speak.

Grace was at work. The experience made me aware of the awkwardness and frustration that people who are physically challenged go through. Years later, I worked in a nursing home and was surprisingly comfortable with stroke victims who could not speak. I talked to them, not expecting a verbal reply, and told them in a normal tone of voice, how I once could not speak and how frustrated I got and they heard me and answered through a nod or a facial expression. Grace prepared me in a special way for this job and allowed patients to connect with someone who genuinely understood because she had had a similar experience.

Probably the largest portion of grace, as a result of my surgery, was generously poured out to my family because, after the surgery, I was no longer allowed to holler. Can you imagine a mother not able to raise her voice? Ever? It took some creative parenting but I had no choice. My family was richly blessed with abundant grace from God when I had throat surgery. My loss was their gain and it lasted their entire childhood.

Paul wrote in *Galatians 1:3,* **Grace and peace to you from God our Father and the Lord Jesus Christ.** Paul was a recipient of God's grace and now he was passing it on to others. He had been a terrible, horrible man of authority who persecuted followers of Christ. Then, God came to Paul in a most dramatic and traumatic manner when He temporarily blinded him and then poured out His grace and Paul's life was forever changed.

Ask God to make you aware of how to pass grace on to others. Compliment a good parent or the person who cleans off tables at the fast food restaurant or who bags your groceries. Grace is not judged by size or importance. It is simply giving and receiving an unexpected gift.

# Burp

STILL NEWLYWEDS, MY husband and I moved to rural California and bought a small house in a small town. We joined a small church with a small congregation and I was anxious to do whatever I could to help it grow and prosper. The "in charge committee," whatever they were called, decided to have a get-together of the congregation and talk about future plans, which included finances. Someone suggested they have a pot-luck dinner first so everyone could get filled to the brim with great food and joyous conversation before being hit with the "facts of life," a proposed budget.

My enthusiasm for everything was apparent so it seemed natural for them to ask me to be in charge of the pot-luck supper. Of course I accepted the challenge, having never done it before. It seemed straight forward; telephone the congregation and ask them to bring a dish to share. Being a newlywed with no children, I didn't know how early some families would arrive or how much teenagers ate. I should have asked them to bring at least two dishes and not to begin eating until a certain time, when most people would be there.

When my husband and I got in line, there were several "pot-luck experts" ahead of us and the serving table was empty. EMPTY! NOTHING! Not even a teaspoon of food remained. People carried their plates past the empty serving table and sat down in dismay.  The man ahead of me in line turned around. I had never met him and he didn't know I was in charge of the food.  He managed a very thin smile and said, "Do you think they will let us go back for firsts?"

# Half Empty, Half Full

MOST OF US know someone who is genuinely depressing. They find fault with almost any subject we bring up. I had a friend like that since the time our children were in preschool together. Since I knew what she was like, I would have a talk with myself before we were getting together and tell myself to not let her get me down. It seldom worked. If I was with her long enough, she won and I departed feeling sad or depressed or downright rotten. She is dead now but my memory of her is of one sad lady.

When we lived in a small Idaho town, a neighbor was confined to home because of poor circulation in her legs but she also had some pretty serious allergies. If I visited and was wearing perfume, she would holler from another room, "Get out! Get out now! I can't stand the smell!" The pastor told us at her funeral that he visited her while she was on her death bed and she beckoned him to come down close to her face so she could talk to him. He thought she wanted to say something relating to her salvation or speak some personal confession so he leaned as far down toward her as he could and she said, "Your after shave is killing me!"

The two people I mentioned never saw their cup as half full. It was always half empty even if they had to empty it out a little to get it that way. Most of us can't really throw stones at this behavior because we are guilty of it ourselves when things just never seem to go right, no matter how hard we think we try, we have a pity party and feel picked on. It is human nature. Scripture tells us in *Isaiah 1:18*, and I paraphrase: **Come now, let us reason together. Think about it. When the worst things happen – when your sins are like scarlet and your cup is half empty, they shall be white as snow and your cup will be overflowing if you are willing and obedient.**

Occasionally, it takes the faith of someone else to remind us of God's abounding love. When I was a child of the Great Depression, I don't remember complaining about the food because children then didn't do that – ever. But, I remember having creamed eggs on toast a lot. And I remember mama smiling and saying "Look at this. Aren't we lucky once again? Some families are going hungry tonight and we have creamed eggs on toast." The tone of her voice described a cup half full.

Sometimes it is our own children who remind us of God's love. Years ago, when we lived in the Sacramento area and our children were still at home, we had a foreign exchange student from Sweden spend a year with us. We decided to take the three girls to Lake Tahoe for the day. A neighbor couple followed us in their car. It was winter but the main highway was open and clear. By the time we started home, it was dark and we had to travel a side road for a few miles. Rounding a turn, we hit black ice and time stood still as we slowly slid out of control, off the road, up an embankment and into a tree. The noise of twisting metal and breaking glass was deafening. Then, there was dead silence. The two older girls were in back with seat belts on. My husband and I also wore seat belts but Julie, age twelve, sat between us where there was no belt so I quickly threw myself over her before the impact. I must have been knocked unconscious because I lost my grip. Julie slid down under the dash board and thought the engine had come in over her. My husband broke the silence. "Is everyone OK?" All answered to the affirmative except Diane who said, "Mom, something is wrong with my back." Diane already had scoliosis – a 20% curvature of her spine. She was under the care of an orthopedic surgeon in Sacramento for this painful condition and exercised daily on special equipment at our home.

Fortunately, our neighbors were following a few minutes behind and, when they came upon us, they immediately transported Diane to the hospital and said they would alert the police. Eventually a tow truck arrived and our friends returned to take us to the hospital. A doctor met us in the waiting room with the sad news that Diane had broken her back. He said she would remain there for a week, then be transported to Sacramento by ambulance and hospitalized for about two weeks. She would be in a full body cast for three months. We followed the doctor to where Diane lay on a gurney in a hallway. She was humming a hymn. I told her what the doctor said. "I don't think so, Mom," she replied. "Call the youth pastor at church and tell him to ask the kids to pray. I think we are going to see a miracle." It was almost midnight. I didn't want to disturb all those people, wondering if it would do any good. My cup was less than half empty because my faith was very shallow. Both of my parents had recently died, my marriage was on the rocks and now Diane had a broken back. Where was God in all this? Not on my side, apparently.

Then reality kicked in. *Come, let us reason together.* Think about it. And I did. In my own pity party, I saw my cup as half empty when Diane was lying there with a broken back and her cup was half full. I remembered Philippians 4:6, **The Lord is near. Do not be anxious about anything but in everything, by prayer and petition, with thanksgiving, present your requests to**

*God.* I called the pastor and he had the youth prayer chain going immediately. That night, at least fifty young people prayed, in obedient faith, for Diane.

Our car had been totaled in the accident so Julie and my husband got a ride home with the neighbors and brought our station wagon back up the mountain early the next day. I spent the night in a nearby motel. The next morning, the doctor took more x-rays and brought them into Diane's room. "I don't know what to say." He began. "I have no explanation for this but there has been a change since last night. I want you to take Diane to the orthopedic doctor already treating her in Sacramento and show him these x-rays."

We didn't need an ambulance. We made a makeshift bed in the back of the station wagon and carefully drove down the mountain. Our Sacramento doctor there looked at the x-rays, had Diane strip down to her underwear and walk away from us. He brought her back and asked her to walk away again while he carefully examined the x-rays. Then, tears appeared in his eyes as he said, "If only surgeons had this skill. Look at this," and he held up the x-rays. "Can you see where the bones here have been crushed? And over here where they appear chipped? And, up here they are crushed again?" Then, he looked directly at Diane. "The break has *cured* your scoliosis. Surgeons do not yet have this skill. I do not know how to do this."

Diane did not go into the hospital for two weeks. She did not have a body cast but was allowed to return to school wearing a brace under her clothing for six weeks. Was this a miracle? We certainly believe it was but it was only one of two. When Diane was in her early 20s, she entered nursing school and one of the criteria for acceptance was a back x-ray to be sure it was strong. Not only did she pass the test, there was no sign of the break.

This did not all happen because of my solid faith. Quite the opposite. My faith at that time was dangerously weakened. My cup was less than half full and nearing empty. I failed to see the good things happening to me. I had two wonderful children, good health and friends who walked through a tough time in my life with me who would not allow me to give up. And now, I had a daughter with every right to throw in the towel and admit defeat. Broken back and all, she saw her cup as half full and filling because she recognized the presence of God and the possibility that a miracle could come from her tragedy. She became the encourager, along with her friends from the youth group, because they believed that God would use this experience to enrich all of our lives through His intervention.

It is human nature to have days when our cup feels half empty but Scripture tells us in *2Corinthians 1:3-4:* **Praise be to the God and Father of our Lord Jesus Christ, the Father of compassion and the God of all comfort, who comforts us in all our troubles, so that we can comfort those in any trouble with the comfort we ourselves have received from God.**

We are bound to encounter trials. A confident faith in God will encourage and strengthen us to endure. I hope you use these scriptures to fill your own cup when it gets low and help others to recognize that your strength comes from faith in the Lord and theirs can, too.

# Gentle Jesus

WHEN WE SAY, "Use me, Lord," and really mean it, we need to be ready for surprises and circumstances we might not have chosen for ourselves. God wants to use us every day in some way; maybe little, insignificant ways. Some Christians think that their only meaningful service to God is by witnessing to their faith and leading others to believe but the Bible tells us that our witness also needs to be in the small stuff. *Matthew 25:34-40* ***Then, the King will say to those on his right, "Come, you who are blessed by my Father; take your inheritance, the kingdom prepared for you since the creation of the world. For I was hungry and you gave me something to eat, I was thirsty and you gave me something to drink, I was a stranger and you invited me in, I needed clothes and you clothed me, I was sick and you looked after me, I was in prison and you came to visit me." Then the righteous will answer him, "Lord, when did we see you hungry and feed you, or thirsty and give you something to drink? When did we see you a stranger and invite you in, or needing clothes and clothe you? When did we see you sick or in prison and go to visit you?" The King will reply, "I tell you the truth, whatever you did for one of the least of these brothers of mine, you did for me."***

Several years ago, I became involved in an organization called Prison Fellowship. It was conceived by Chuck Colson, who had been an advisor to President Nixon. Chuck Colson was involved in the Watergate Affair where several of Nixon's staff broke into the office of the Democratic Party. They were caught, tried in court and Colson was among those sent to prison. God did not let him off lightly. *Galatians 6:3,* **If anyone thinks he is something when he is nothing, he deceives himself.** God allowed Colson to be incarcerated in order to shake him up and help him see himself as anything *but* the powerful person he believed himself to be. He was a common criminal. God treated him with punishment. While there, he had time to observe the prison system and its inadequacies. After his release, Colson accepted Christ and felt a calling to dedicate his life to improving the prison system in practical ways and also bring the word of God to prisoners. He started the Angel Tree project where, at Christmas time, people purchase gifts for the children of prisoners. He introduced marriage counseling to prisoners about to be released, and to their wives. The majority of prisoners, who attend Prison Fellowship classes prior to release, do not return to prison. These practices are being used around the world and they are working because the love of God is the basis for all the teaching.

Colson had a religious experience that put him at the feet of Jesus in humble submission and Gentle Jesus showed him how he could be a *powerful servant* for the rest of his life. Gentle Jesus took this man who had been reduced to nothing and made him the head of what is now an international organization that brings the word of God to prisoners in an every-day, practical manner. When Colson thought he was somebody special, he was nothing. When he accepted his *nothingness*, Gentle Jesus raised him up to be the leader of thousands; maybe millions.

My involvement with Prison Fellowship included answering prisoner mail and led me to an ex-con by the name of Jerry Graham. Jerry was a smooth persuader and used this talent to cheat people and perpetrate many crimes. Society punished him by sending him to prison. Jerry accepted Christ and later wrote a book about his experience. At the end of the book, he invited any reader to write to him at a PO Box. He thought he might get one or two letters a month but hundreds of letters poured in from prisoners and I became one of the volunteers who answered the mail. When I was invited to participate in this ministry, I have to admit I took a while to think it over and pray for some direction. I had the usual pre-conceived ideas of what a prisoner was; a hardened criminal who had done some hideous crime. Most of the men and women who wrote had made some bad choices that resulted in a prison sentence. They were anxious to return to free society and get on with their lives. Often, they wrote that their mothers and grandmothers prayed for them daily and that gave them comfort.

Each letter we wrote back contained a message of encouragement and hope through Christ. We never signed our last name or gave our return address. Prison Fellowship paid the postage. Often, I answered twenty letters a week and this ministry went on for several years. It was not a job I sought. I prayed that I would know what to say, not be afraid, and do it well. Gentle Jesus guided me in such a way that I felt OK about writing to prisoners. I wasn't nervous. I followed the rules and hoped my efforts would help the prisoners to get through a difficult time. My involvement with Prison Fellowship continued in a Bible Study for the wives of prisoners. I was not the leader. I was just another wife, there to study and learn and have fellowship together.

One day, I received a telephone call from someone in the Prison Fellowship office. "We have the wife and child of a prisoner coming to town from southern California," she said. "The woman has so little money; all she can afford is gas, nothing for food or lodging. The woman and her son are coming to visit her husband in Folsom Prison. They can only see him for one day." There was a hesitation. Then the caller asked, "Would you and your husband be willing to let this lady and her son stay overnight with you, feed them supper and also breakfast the next day?" I was shocked that we were asked to have personal contact with a prisoner's family. In the letters I wrote to prisoners, I could not even mention my last name, let alone give out my address. Now, I am asked to provide bed and breakfast to family members. What could I say? I told her I would talk to my husband and get back to her. When I called him at work, he was hesitant and less than enthusiastic. He asked what I thought and I said I was willing to try it and believed Prison Fellowship would not ask something of us that was uncomfortable or dangerous. He hesitantly agreed and I called the lady back. *Proverbs 3:5-6,* ***Trust in the Lord with all your heart and lean not on your own understanding; in all your ways acknowledge Him, and He will make your paths straight.*** I had two days to stew over this and didn't waste a minute. What was I thinking? How could I have invited a perfect stranger and her child to share our home? What if they stole something? Then I began to wonder what they looked like. For a person who considered herself tolerant and not prejudice, my imagination went crazy. By the time her car pulled up in front of our house, I was worn out.

My husband, Lowell, and I stepped outside to greet them. The car door opened and out stepped a petite, neatly dressed woman in her mid thirties with a sweet little boy who stayed close to her. My only thought was, "Gentle Jesus, you are so good to me. All my insecurities and worries were for nothing." We all introduced ourselves. Their names were Carol and Bobby. Lowell took her one small suitcase for the two of them and we ushered them into our house and to their room. It didn't take long to get acquainted and, while we were eating supper, she told us about her husband. "He was the pastor of a small church," she said. Again, I thought, "Jesus, you are so gentle to me. You are making this so easy for me." She continued, "He got involved in some kind of a real estate deal that was shady and now he is in a minimum security part of the prison for eighteen months. It has been several months since we have seen him and we miss him so much." She went on to say that she was working a minimum wage job. She didn't complain but it was apparent that the salary was not meeting their basic needs. She did not ask for financial help and we did not offer any. After supper, Carol and I were clearing the table while Lowell and Bobby talked in the living room. Soon, they came to us and announced that they wanted to go to the demolition derby in another town nearby. "Oh, please, Mommy, can I go?" Bobby begged and Carol agreed. No one was more surprised than me. Lowell *never* went to the car races but he saw the ad in the paper and thought it would be a great "grandpa" type event and off they went. Again, I thought about Gentle Jesus and how He gave Lowell just the right idea for the circumstance. They wouldn't have to carry on an awkward conversation all evening. They could watch the cars and then have something to talk about.

This also gave Carol and me time together and she told me about their life in the ministry; how it seemed so good in many ways but how it was financially difficult because they had a small congregation in a rural area. Somehow, her husband heard of a way to get some quick cash that resulted in his being arrested for fraud. The experience was humiliating for the couple and their son, but she said the most heartbreaking part of this experience was the betrayal felt by much of the congregation. A few of them were forgiving souls and stayed by her while she waited for her husband to return home. She didn't cry while she told me the story. She had great composure but I could see the hurt in her eyes and hear it in her voice. All the while, I prayed in my mind, "Gentle Jesus, help me to say the right thing, even if the right thing is nothing."

The guys got home late but we waited up to hear all about the evening. There was no sleeping-in the next morning because they had only one day to spend with their husband and dad. Each moment was precious. I fed them a big, nourishing breakfast and packed enough food for two more meals into their cooler. Then, they were gone and we never saw them again. She did send a thank-you note to say they had a good, but short, visit with her husband and made it home safely. There was no return address.

God gives us opportunities to serve Him in big and little ways. Sometimes it is so insignificant; we hardly recognize this as part of a plan. That is why we should never think of any day as *just one more uneventful, boring day.* You may have a conversation with someone that encourages them or helps them in the smallest way by giving a smile or a compliment.

There are two things I like to do, write and cook. I wrote letters to prisoners and cooked an occasional meal for a stranger. God took these abilities and used them in special ways. It was no hardship for me. These were simply ordinary acts done by ordinary people for ordinary people. Probably, neither you nor I could conduct a Billy Graham crusade but Jesus tells us that, when we tend to the *small stuff,* it's like we're doing it for Him. I am in awe that the basic advice we are given in the Bible, written so long ago, is applicable today. We might update it because of changes in our life style or technology that wasn't around when the original script was written but the concept is the same and that is where the Bible is so appropriate to any time in history. In today's world, we might say, "Lord, when did I text you or e-mail you or send you a letter of encouragement on Facebook? When did I listen to you? When did I recognize that you needed help I could not give and supplied some resources? When did I have the courage to meet a new friend or invite someone to my home?" And, of course, the answer is that when we do these things for anyone else, we are doing it for the Lord.

Perhaps you will have the opportunity to do something for someone you will never see again. I am paraphrasing *Hebrews 13: 1-2,* **Keep on loving each other as brothers. Do not forget to entertain new acquaintances for, by so doing, some people have entertained angels without knowing it.**

# Set Apart

CAN YOU REMEMBER circumstances from your past where you felt insignificant? Was it when you started a new job, a new school or encountered an uncomfortable social situation? For me, it was looking around at the grandeur and magnificence of this world and thinking, "I am nothing." God tells us in the Bible that it is just the opposite. He says you and I are this important: *Jer. 1:5,* **Before I formed you in the womb, I knew you. Before you were born, I set you apart.** Can you believe that, with all the people in the world, God chose to set *us* apart?

When I was nine years old, I stayed the summer with friends in Rochester, MN and I spent a lot of time listening to the radio. It was before TV and during the Great Depression. There were no talk shows on the radio and no advice programs. There were many soap operas like Ma Perkins and Stella Dallas. There was news and an occasional speech by President Roosevelt which they called a Fireside Chat but mostly, there was music, all kinds of music; songs from WWI (My Buddy), songs from the turn of the century (Daisy, Daisy) and there were hymns, lots of hymns. We didn't have Praise Songs as we know them today but we did have Gospel, which were snappy hymns and we had what we called Negro Spirituals, songs of oppression during slavery that spoke of a better life to come in heaven.

That summer, for whatever reason I could not understand, I learned many tunes and most of the verses as I sang along with the radio programs. I remember wondering why. Why was I so passionate about learning those songs when none of my friends knew them? My family wasn't musical. My Father whistled a lot but he always ended with a different song than the one he started with. All these songs were tucked away in my mind for many years before I understood why I had learned them. I didn't know much about God at that time but He knew all about me.

Thirty-five years later, I got a job as an activities director in a nursing home. One of the residents' favorite activities was the weekly sing-along. Some of those patients were born at the turn of the century and lived during WWI. They loved the music of that era. Sometimes they needed help with the tune or a jump start with the words and who knew them all? Me! The sing-along was therapeutically satisfying. Patients who had little other movement would tap the arm of their wheelchairs in time to the music. They enjoyed reality orientation while reminiscing. As I led the music, it was clear to me that God had prepared me for this moment thirty-five years earlier. I was serving Him by serving them. *He had set me apart.*

I believe we are not prepared to do just one thing well but that we have many possibilities of service. In 1973, we moved to a rural area of Northern California and, for reasons I could not explain, I became interested in the names of streets and roads in the area. Where did they lead? What streets did they cross? I was so fascinated that, when I had extra time, I would drive around randomly, memorizing the street names. Then, I joined the volunteer rescue squad at our rural fire department. I had a map book and a radio receiver in my home and, when there was an emergency, the dispatcher would alert me.

He gave a brief description of the emergency, along with the address and cross street. I knew exactly where to go without spending precious time on the map book. I believe God prepared me to serve Him the very best way I could by creating in me a curiosity about location of streets and roads. *God had set me apart.*

These experiences will not bring me pictures in the paper or public applause. We do not need applause from people when we know we are already a success in God's eyes because He has set us apart to do His will. Sometimes we get stuck in past accomplishments that we did well and think that is all we can do when God really wants us to move on. Years ago I taught nursery school. I helped to raise foster children and felt that I did these things well but it is a different time and place now. I no longer have the same energy or desire to do those tasks.

Before my husband, Lowell, and I were married, he told me that he wanted his son and daughter from a previous marriage to live with him some day. "Fat chance!" I thought. Their mother was taking good care of them and I dismissed the idea until the children, not yet teenagers, expressed a desire to live with us. One Friday when Lowell and I thought he was picking them up for the weekend, he arrived at their house and found them, along with their belongings in boxes in the front yard. Their mother agreed to let them move.

I watched from our kitchen window as they pulled up in the station wagon and began unloading box after box and a dog, and I battled God in my mind. "I cannot, I CAN NOT do this," I argued. "I raised foster children for fifteen years and it was hard and I wasn't planning on this." Then, for reasons unknown, I went from panic to peace. It was as if something said, "Those years were preparing you for this." I went outside, grabbed a box in one arm and the dog in the other and walked in the house, knowing my life would never be the same. Like every family, there were good and bad days, good and bad years, but we grew to love each other with a strong bond that remains today. I am richly blessed and more complete because of them.

An example of God preparing me for something in the distant future is when I received a phone call asking me to come out of retirement for a while and become the chaplain for a new hospice starting in our area. These people didn't open the phone book and randomly select a name with their eyes closed and say, "Let's call her." Without them knowing it, or me knowing it, I believe this was part of God's plan to set me apart long ago and prepare me over the years. Twenty five years earlier, I took my first hospice training. Afterward, I was employed in a hospice for ten years and volunteered for fifteen. During that time, I also spent a year in study through a seminary, not learning theology but a curriculum called Human Values. It changed my life. I cannot translate Greek or Hebrew. I cannot interpret Biblical philosophy, but I can relate teachings from the Bible to everyday life. Being a chaplain was a natural transition.

Think about the many ways God prepared you for the events of your life; how He protected you from making wrong decisions when you trusted Him. Think of the times you wanted control and the times you gave the control to God. Think of some of the things you have done well and then let them go so you can be open to what He is preparing you for up ahead. He tells us as much in *Romans 12:12*, **be glad for all God is planning for you.** Do you realize that you are in the process of being prepared right now? As we fulfill one purpose, He prepares us for the next one. Circumstances may be wonderful or difficult, disappointing or elating. During all these experiences, God promises you that He will never leave you or forsake you. Remember that He knew you before you were formed in the womb and *set you apart* before you were born.

# Prayer Changes Things

GRANDMA LIVED WITH us when I was young. It was our turn. With no Welfare, Social Security or Medicare, responsibility for elderly parents fell onto the adult children. Aunt Lil cared for her for a number of years. When the State Bank in Stewartville, Minnesota closed during the Great Depression, my Dad, the bank bookkeeper, was out of work so we moved to Rochester where he could not find a job either. We moved to Minneapolis and shared one portion of a fourplex apartment with Aunt Lil, her daughter and Grandma. Dad found a steady job and, after two years, saved enough money to rent an apartment upstairs in a house for our family of three. Grandma moved with us and occupied the second bedroom while I slept in an alcove off the living room. It did not have closets or doors but it was mine. I no longer had to share a bed with my cousin.

Grandma had few personal possessions. Her Bible was in large print but her eyesight was so poor she no longer could read it so I read it to her every night. Considering the fact that it was in the Swedish language, that was quite a fete but I read phonetically and she often replied with a "Ya, ya," and a smile. I must have been doing something right. Grandma's other possession was a wooden plaque that hung by her bedroom door and, in English said, "Prayer Changes Things." She lived by that motto and, often, when I entered her room, she was praying.

Her example taught me that prayer was part of every-day life.

There are people who doubt the reality of prayer and others who consider it hogwash. Some scientists prefer to ignore anything spiritual but others are fascinated by results of faith-based healing. A cardiologist at a University Medical Center in the South conducted a global study on spirituality in healing of heart patients. At a Mid-America heart institute, two cardiologists conducted a study on 1000 heart patients who did not know that half the patients were being prayed for by the hospital chaplain and a group of volunteers and the other half were not being prayed for. The results were that those prayed for had fewer heart attacks, strokes, and life-threatening complications than those not prayed for. The same results happened with AIDS patients who were studied. Even the scientific community is baffled. The Mayo Clinic and other well-known medical institutions have information available in their publications regarding prayer as a support to healing. The medical community is paying attention. In fact, for a Hospice to become Medicare Certified, it has to include the services of a chaplain on its team.

As Christians, we say we believe in prayer but, when it is answered, we are surprised. Is it because we cannot see God so we find it hard to accept His reality? We cannot see electricity and yet, when we push a button or flip the switch, we expect the light to go on or the computer to boot up or the curling iron to heat. Some people put more faith in electricity than in prayer and yet prayer is so much more powerful. Prayer is linked to faith. *Hebrews 11:1,* **Now faith is being sure of what we hope for and certain of what we do not see.**

Sometimes, God's answer is different from what we thought about or planned. We are so restricted in our humanness that it is hard for us to "think outside the box," and God surprises us. I have a friend who was hanging out with the wrong crowd, abusing alcohol and getting in trouble with the law. I invited him to church more than once but he turned me down. I told him I was going to pray for him daily, that he would meet different friends and develop new interests. I imagined him connecting with some fellow who liked to fish and hunt, play pool and stay out of trouble. I kept my promise and prayed daily. It took longer than I hoped but, one day, he happily told me that he had a new friend. "Does he fish and hunt and play pool?" I asked. "She plays pool," he replied. "She?" I asked. "It's a female friend?" "Yes," he replied, "and she's a Christian." "What a God," I thought. I never even considered a lady friend and she has been such a positive influence on his life. God honored my prayer but, while I stayed safely inside the box, He ventured out and found the perfect friend.

I have been brought to my knees in humility over the faith of children in my life. When my oldest daughter was two years old, our first foster children came to live with us. Richard was nine and his half-sister, Barbara, was seven. They had an older brother in another foster home and a younger sister who remained with the mother. The social worker drove into our driveway and these two scrawny little kids got out of the car, each carrying a paper grocery bag that contained their worldly possessions and clothes. That first night, as the three children were ready for bed, I asked Richard and Barbara if they knew about prayer. "Oh yes," Richard replied, "I know the Lord's prayer." He began to recite. "Our Father who art in heaven, Hollywood be thy name." I knew my work was cut out for me. Barbara gave sentence prayers about anything and everything. Richard always prayed the same prayer, night after night. "God, please make my daddy kind to other people."

The children did well in school, joined the Scouts and attended Sunday School. Weeks and months passed and Richard's prayer remained the same. As he developed a trust in me, he began to share about what an angry and punishing man his dad was; beating the boys with his belt and actually hanging them from large hooks on the wall. One day, after an especially painful beating, the two boys decided to run away. They each had less than a dollar in change and spent that on ice cream. They slept on the bank of the Sacramento River and ate grass. After two days, they were cold and hungry and afraid to return home so they stopped a police car and told them what happened. As a result, the two boys and Barbara were placed in foster homes. When Richard told me his story, I felt ill. I told him that I didn't know if he would ever see his dad again but that I believed God heard his prayer.

Richard had a stronger faith than me. One day I was struck speechless when the social worker called to say that the children's father was in the area and wanted to see them. She would pick them up the following Saturday and I was welcome to ride along if I wished. The ride over to another part of Sacramento was tense for all of us but, once inside the house, the children's father made us feel comfortable and spoke quietly to each child. This man had no resemblance to the angry, mean person the children told me about. When it came time to leave, Richard walked over to his dad, put his arms around him and said, "I can hardly believe this is really you."

The ride home was a reflective one for Richard and me. Barbara sat up front and chattered all the way. Richard and I sat in the back seat and thought about what we had just experienced. He was at great peace because what he believed would happen did happen. He believed that in some mysterious way, which he did not understand and did not need to understand, God answered his prayer. I was totally humbled by the experience and ashamed at my own doubting. It took a scrawny little boy to show me the reality of complete faith, without question. What I learned from a little boy was that, indeed, prayer changes things. It changed a daddy… and it changed me.

The children were only with us for six months before their mother moved away and wanted them close to her. Having them leave us was one of the most difficult experiences I ever had and we were directed by the Agency to not have any contact with them. I tried hard to work through the grief but it took a long time. However, Barbara did contact me many years later and we had a wonderful reunion. I will tell you about that later in the book.

# Never Alone

JOHN THE BAPTIST had been beheaded. When Jesus heard about it, He took a boat to a secluded place in order to be alone and reflect on what happened but He no longer could hide from the people. As soon as someone heard where He was, people began to gather from all around to listen to Him and bring their sick for healing. About 5000 men gathered, as well as women and children, according to Matthew. There could easily have been 15,000 people there. Jesus had compassion on them and met their needs, eventually feeding them from a small picnic of five loaves and two fish. Obviously, everyone, including the disciples, marveled and they were confused as to how Jesus made this happen.

Then, He sent them on ahead while he sought a quiet retreat. *Matthew 14:22-26,* **Immediately Jesus made the disciples get into the boat and go on ahead of him to the other side, while he dismissed the crowd. After he had dismissed them, he went up on a mountainside by himself to pray. When evening came, he was there alone, but the boat was already a considerable distance from land, buffeted by the waves because the wind was against it. During the fourth watch of the night Jesus went out to them, walking on the lake. When the disciples saw him walking on the lake, they were terrified. "It's a ghost." they said and cried out in fear. But Jesus** *immediately said to them: "Take courage! It is I. Don't be afraid.*

They were seasoned fishermen and yet this storm was like no other. The waves beat over the boat and they feared capsizing. Then, to compound their fear, Jesus came to them, walking on the water, and the Bible tells us they thought they were seeing a ghost and were terrified. Have you ever been terrified? I tried to think back on circumstances in my own past and decided I never had that awful experience. I have had my share of fear. I have been in a couple serious auto accidents but everything happened so fast I didn't seem to have time to be terrified. For me, terror would have to include fear of impending death and I think this is what the disciples felt. They were on their own and whatever skills they collectively had, it wasn't enough to save them from impending doom. They were about to drown. Then, they saw something even more frightening than the water that was about to consume them. They saw what they thought was a ghost. *Matthew 14:27,* **But immediately Jesus spoke to them saying, "Be of good cheer! It is I; do not be afraid".** Jesus did not wait or put them to a test. As soon as He saw their terror, He identified himself and calmed them.

Let's fast forward to another story. Jesus has completed His ministry, been falsely accused, tried, crucified and laid in the tomb. It's the third day after His death and two of his followers are on a several mile walk home from Jerusalem to the town of Emmaus. They can't stop talking about what happened earlier and repeat to each other, "Some women went to the tomb and said Jesus wasn't there and an angel spoke to them. How can this be? Maybe they were so upset, they didn't know what they really saw. And yet, some men went to the tomb and said it was as the women told them. It's all so confusing and such a mystery." Read *Luke 24.*

What thread of commonality runs through these two accounts; the apostles fearing death by drowning and the men returning to Emmaus? It is this: Jesus was with the people in both accounts well before they recognized His presence. When the fishermen were floundering in the rugged water, when they felt sure they were going to drown, when they saw Jesus but didn't recognize Him at a distance, everything seemed hopeless. They had lost control of the boat. They were much too far from shore to swim. They saw no way out. Then, they recognized Jesus and their *hopelessness* immediately turned to *hopefulness* for they knew that Jesus' very presence represented promise and safety.

The men on the road to Emmaus were focused on one thing. Failure! The man whom they thought was the long awaited Messiah was dead. This Jesus performed miracles such as had never been witnessed before. He healed the sick, caused the blind to see and the lame to walk and He actually raised someone from the dead. And now, *He* was dead and they were very sad and sorry. What looked like the revelation of prophesy, the coming of the Messiah, turned out to be a huge disappointment. The dead body was lowered from the cross and all the hopes and dreams of a nation were buried with it in the tomb.

Now, the tomb was empty and He was missing. The Bible says that Jesus himself, the risen Lord, came up and walked along with the men but they were kept from recognizing Him. It doesn't say, "God blinded their eyes from recognizing Him." Perhaps it was more like what we sometimes experience today when someone we love dies and we think we see them in a crowd or at WalMart or in a passing car. For a fleeting moment, we almost stop breathing because we so want it to be true. Then, reality kicks in and we know it was not them because they died. These men may have thought the fellow traveler resembled Jesus but reality reminded them that it couldn't be Him because Jesus died.

Just as the living Jesus saw (from a distance) the fear and anguish of the fishermen and went to them, even though they didn't recognize Him, so the risen Jesus saw the grief and sadness of the men on the road and went to them and at first, they didn't recognize Him. He allowed the fishermen to express their terror and calmed the water. He enlightened the men on the road with prophesy, reminding them that what happened to Jesus had been foretold.

Then, in a common, ordinary act of breaking bread and giving it to them, He revealed himself as the risen Christ. Perhaps it was in the unique way he broke the bread that identified Him as the real Jesus. You know how it is with people in your life who do or say things in some personal way that sets them apart in your mind. It is like a fingerprint that solely identifies them. Can you still hear your mother saying, "Bring a sweater. I don't want you to catch cold?" Or dad reminding you to, "Do it well so you will not look back with regret." Is there someone in your life who has quoted a certain saying ever since you can remember and, when you hear it, that person pops into your mind? Maybe Jesus had such a unique, personal way to share the Lord's Supper that when He gave thanks and broke that bread, immediately they recognized Him as the *risen* Christ, not the dead and broken body they saw on the cross. Immediately, he disappeared and the men were so excited, they hurried back to Jerusalem to tell the others.

Do you feel you have to be in trouble, or frightened or helpless before Jesus turns up in your life? Is it only when you are grieving or confused or doubtful that you finally feel His presence? Perhaps it's because *you* have pulled away. Jesus wants to quiet the difficult times for you and tell you He is near. In fact, He promised to never leave us alone. He didn't say He would send us a friend. He didn't say He would send us a servant. He said he would send us a *comforter,* a spiritual form of himself. When you lose your job, when your health fails, when someone disappoints you, He is there. You never have to bear the burden of fear or helplessness or inadequacy alone. Recognize the reality of Jesus' presence in the form of the Holy Spirit and invite Him into your life and into your needs.

# Five — Letter Words

LET US LOOK at some five-letter words in our language that are worth examining. The first five-letter word is **Worry**. We are all familiar with it. Some of us are experts at it. Some of us are "professional worriers." It's our job!

Worry has to do with the future. We never worry about the past except for how it will affect the future. Do you know what the Bible says about worry? *Matt. 6: 25-31,* **Therefore I tell you, do not worry about your life, what you will eat or drink, or about your body, what you will wear. Is not life more important than food, and the body more important than clothes? Look at the birds of the air; they do not sow or reap or store away in barns, and yet your heavenly Father feeds them. Are you not much more valuable than they? Who of you by worrying can add a single hour to his life?"** Worry may actually shorten your life. Medical science has proven that worry can lead to stroke or stomach problems or other internal disorders because our physical health is directly related to emotional wellness. How do we stop worrying when we, or someone else, is failing at school or on drugs or just lost a job or is ill or in financial struggles?

Several years ago one of my daughters, you guessed it, number two, called me late at night, completely distraught. I can't remember the problem now but she was totally beside herself to where I was concerned for her safety. I wondered if she might be suicidal. I chose to take her despair upon myself and stayed awake all night, often on my knees in prayer for her safety. I literally worried myself sick. The next morning I called her, fully expecting a stranger to answer the phone and tell me she was dead. Instead, *she* answered with a cheerful, "Hi, Mom." I almost whispered, "You were so distraught last night, I worried terribly and spent much of the night on my knees in prayer for you. Are you all right?" "Oh, Mom," she replied, "I'm fine. Once I had a good night's sleep, the problem took care of itself. I'm sorry I put you through that." Now that I realized she was not dead, I wanted to kill her (figure of speech). I felt like I had shortened my own life by worrying so much and made a pact with myself never to do that again for anyone. It didn't help her and got me nowhere. I decided that, if a similar experience happened, I would express my sincere concern, offer helpful resources if that was applicable but would not take on the problem. I needed an alternative plan.

What if we changed worry into concern? Worry leads us down a hopeless dead-end path. There is no answer. No change. Just more worry. When we worry, we're like gerbils in a cage, running round and round, faster and faster, wearing ourselves out and getting nowhere. We stop for a short rest and start up again, always with the same result.

*Concern* has possibilities. Concern has hope. Concern recognizes that we may be or feel helpless but not hopeless. When we pray a worry prayer it is negative, headed downhill. "Lord, I'm so worried, I'm ill. I can't sleep. The problem is beyond my reach. Please change things. Please do this or that. I'm so distressed, I can't think straight any more." When we pray a prayer of concern, we release the control to God which immediately frees our body to relax. "Lord, I commit (.........) to your care. I know that you honor my prayer and concern and my act of intercession on their behalf. I ask that you draw him/her close to you and protect and direct them. I ask that you bring a peaceful conclusion to the problem. Lord, if I can serve you in any way, use me. Make your desire clear to me. I commit my concern to you in total trust."

The next five-letter word is **Trust**. The dictionary interprets trust as *"the firm reliance on the integrity or ability of a person or thing."* What does the Bible say about trust? Psalm 119:105, **Thy word is a lamp unto my feet and a light unto my path.** In other words, by trusting God's word, He promises to lead us, one step at a time. It is only when we try to see into the future that we worry because it is darkness, unknown, out of our control and we feel helpless. When we trust the future to God, and are willing to follow one step at a time, knowing that He has complete control of each next step, we are free to live a healthier, more peaceful life than one of worry, worry, worry.

God's word is a lamp unto our feet so we can be absolutely sure of the next step. If he gave us a spotlight into our future, we might panic and say, "That's too difficult. That's too painful. I can't handle that." But, with only a lamp to guide our next step we can trust that whatever comes will also be manageable. It all hinges on trust.

Our third and final five-letter word is **Faith**. The dictionary expresses faith as, *confident belief or trust in a person, idea, or thing.* The Bible explains faith like this: *Hebrews 11:1-3,* **Now faith is being sure of what we hope for and certain of what we do not see. This is what the ancients were commended for. By faith we understand that the universe was formed at God's command so that what is seen was not made out of what was visible.** In a very practical way, He tells us in *Matthew 11:28-30,* **Come to me, all you who are weary and burdened, and I will give you rest. Take my yoke upon you and learn from me for I** *am gentle and humble in heart and you will find rest for your souls. For my yoke is easy and my burden is light.* The yoke is a curved frame used to couple draft animals which makes the work easier. Symbolically speaking, Jesus says, "Yoke up with me and we will go through this life together.

We do this every day with our own children. We assure them that we love them and want to protect them and keep them safe. We ask them to share their problems and concerns with us and, when they do, we offer advice or just listen. If we can do that in a human way with our children, we should be able to trust our heavenly Father just as our children trust us. Our relationship with God is very real. It is just not visual. That is where the faith we read about in Hebrews comes in.

# Armistice Day

I READ RECENTLY about a special day in the history of our country, indeed the world. On the 11th hour of the 11th day of the 11th month in the year 1918, there was a temporary cessation of hostilities between the Allies and the Germans. They agreed to *peacefully* disagree until a final treaty, called the Treaty of Versailles, was signed June 28, 1919 to end the Great War, World War I. No one could imagine a greater war. This cease in hostilities was called an armistice.

When we look at conflict on a global scale, it is almost impossible to comprehend but when we view it on a personal level, it's perfectly understandable. Small spats become hurtful insults that become such bad behavior we're ashamed to admit to it. Where does this behavior come from? We don't start out the day intending to hurt someone. We want to be kind and respectful and suddenly something doesn't go our way or we feel we are losing control for some reason and we lash out before they can lash out at us.

Perhaps global conflict begins in this very manner, individuals seeking personal power. Does the Bible speak to this problem? You bet it does! While it sits on our coffee tables collecting dust, or tucked away on a book shelf so as not to get soiled, it cries out to us, "Open me. Trust me. I have news for you that will change your life and give you peace." If you don't know where to start, go to the New Testament and start with the Gospel of John. As you read a little each day, the books that follow will speak to you and your needs.

The Apostle, Paul enjoyed teaching through letter writing to Christians in various cities like Ephesus, Corinth and Rome. What if we could correspond with him today? How would he respond to our questions about conflict, especially *inner* conflict? All of the answers you hear are directly from a Bible in modern English. You will find that they apply as directly today as they did when written.

Dear Paul, Greetings from (your town). I hope you can help us solve our conflicts. I also speak for others when I say I cannot seem to do what I know is right. I get upset when I shouldn't. I holler when I don't want to. How about it, Paul, do you have any good advice?

*Dear (town) - I'm in the same boat as you. This is what I wrote to the Romans. (Romans 7:15)* **I do not understand what I do. For what I want to do I do not do but what I hate, I do.**

Dear Paul, We are bound by experiences from our past. We are shackled to old wounds that no longer have power over us. We don't want to be slaves to the past because it robs us of freedom we should be enjoying today but, even today brings its share of heartaches. We grieve losses; loss of a loved one, loss of eyesight or hearing, loss of a job, loss of the freedom to drive, loss of a friendship. Can you give us a few words of comfort here?

*Dear Friends, This is how I addressed the Romans when they wrote about loss. (Romans 8:18)* **For I consider that the sufferings of this present time are not worthy to be compared with the glory which shall be revealed in us.**

Dear Paul, All that we have shared with you boils down to trusting God for the right answers but that is not always easy.

Sometimes, we don't even know how to pray.

*Dear (town), I understand and this is what I believe. Romans 8:38-39,* **For I am persuaded that neither death nor life nor angels nor principalities nor things present nor things to come, nor height nor depth nor any other created thing shall be able to separate us from the love of God**

Paul is right. No matter how sincere we are about wanting to do the right thing, no matter how good our intentions are, we stumble and fall. Then, we beat ourselves up because we know our lower nature is winning the battle of our will. It is then that we are reminded of Paul's understanding and love for the Romans, and for us. We thank God and start over.

Perhaps that's how the Armistice worked. Nations bowed to their lower nature. They became greedy and willing to hurt others and destroy their land and possessions in order to gain power illegally and, as they fought, they realized their errors and compromised enough to end the bloodshed and destruction. They agreed to find a peaceful way to move ahead.

Do you suppose that's how God wants us to treat conflict? Every one of us has made mistakes, sometimes monumental mistakes -- usually with our tongue. We say very hurtful things to others in anger, in a lie or fabrication. Sometimes, someone hurts us. Looking back, we understand what Paul wrote to the Romans when he said our lower nature takes over. We know we cannot take back our ugly words and we grieve that such language ever left our lips.

How can we move on? First, by asking forgiveness from the persons we offended. Hopefully, they will say "yes" but, if they say "no, I will never forgive you," then, that becomes their problem. As embarrassing and humbling it is to seek forgiveness, when we have done it sincerely, we have fulfilled our commitment. As difficult as asking forgiveness is, it is easier for some of us than forgiving. When we have been abused, we often desire revenge. *Revenge is like taking poison and hoping the other guy dies.* The very act of forgiveness can free us up to emotional and spiritual recovery.

Can this be *your* Armistice Day? Can you say, "Enough is enough! My attitude is getting me nowhere. I'm sick and tired of spinning my wheels. Maybe it's time to compromise, agree to peacefully disagree, seek forgiveness and forgive."

Congratulations! Happy Armistice Day!

# Second Burp

OUR CHURCH HIRED a new Education Director. After a couple of weeks into the job, I was chatting with him in his office. He lamented, "I'm having a problem remembering names. The congregation has only one name to remember. Mine. I have to remember all of them and I'm not doing too well."

Smugly, I mentioned a fool-proof method of remembering and that was by association. "Just associate the new word with one you are familiar with," I said, and continued, "I will never forget your name, Mr. Lovit." "My name is Huggett," he replied.

# Unconditional Love

WHOEVER COINED THE saying, "Parenting is not for sissies," hit the nail on the head. However hard we try, even our best of intentions do not always result in happy endings. When daughter number two was in her early teens, she tried my patience to the limit. While away from home for a while, she poured her anger into a letter telling me what a rotten mother I was. At the end she wrote, "PS: send cookies." She obviously rebelled at my parenting skills but knew, without a doubt, that my love was unconditional.

Today, at age 50+, she is the one child who calls me most often to make sure I am OK. She trusted my love, and now I trust her devotion. As an adult, she raised two good sons and realized that parenting was like a rollercoaster, ups and downs. When I answered the phone, to hear her voice during her child rearing years, it was often for advice or encouragement. As children of God, we are assured that He is constant; the same yesterday, today, and tomorrow. We can count on Him; the only one who will never leave us.

Even in adulthood, we rely on our living parents for advice or direction. In the early 1950s, my husband and I moved from Minnesota to California where he found employment after college. Life was good and, at $330 a month, we felt on our way to financial success. Just one problem interrupted our plans. After extended medical assistance and a variety of uncomfortable tests, we learned that we could not have children of our own. I was heartbroken. Both my husband and I loved children and wanted a big family. I felt betrayed by God because I had poured out my heart's desires to Him in full confidence that it was just a matter of time until these dreams would be realized. I wrote my mother a tearful account of the doctor's findings. In her wisdom, mother replied, "I am so sorry that you cannot have children of your own. I looked forward to being a Grandma but I want to remind you that many of your friends have husbands fighting in Korea right now. They may come home mentally or physically damaged or they may not return home at all. You have a husband with you to share your life. Appreciate that and enjoy each other. Do your best to move ahead and the future will take care of itself." What wise council.

I wanted to move back to family and friends who would console and encourage me so I wrote to my father and asked him to loan us the money to move. We had already accumulated our share of worldly goods since settling in California. When we moved out west, everything fit into the car. Now, we needed a trailer to accommodate the return home. I was their only child, the apple of my father's eye, but he put his own feelings aside and came up with a brilliant idea. Because he could see the broad picture and possibilities of a successful future for us in California, he wrote that he would gladly send us the money to move back *in a year*. He went on to say that, giving any change a year to prove itself was a good idea, whether it was a move or a job or any other life-altering decision. If, in a year, we still felt that moving back to Minnesota was right, he would loan us the money. That was not the answer I hoped for but I trusted his judgment and, of course, we settled into making a home for ourselves in California and began the process of adopting our first child.

As I look upon these events, I relate them to how our Heavenly Father cares so deeply for you and me. He listens to us and wants only the best for us but sometimes the answer is "not yet." Our Heavenly Father sees the big picture while we are looking through a very limited knothole. However, if we can trust Him, we know that the outcome will be what we hoped for or even better.

When my daughter, Diane, broke her back in an auto accident, she didn't ask me to pray. She asked me to call her youth group to pray and they did and she was miraculously healed. When my foster son, Richard, prayed for his Daddy who beat him and hung him from hooks on the wall, he asked God to make his Daddy kind to others. Our Heavenly Father allowed us to see the man, after months of prayers, and witness to his change in behavior from a very *mean* person to a very *kind* one. God honored Richard's faith and trust and prayers for this man.

The Bible tells us of the crippled man who wanted to be healed and how he and his friends were sure that Jesus could do this. The friends took tiles off the roof of a house where Jesus was and lowered the cripple, on his mat, into the room. Jesus healed the man, not only because of his own faith but because of the faith of his friends. Even today, we support each other through our actions or our prayers.

There was a blind man from birth who believed that Jesus could heal him and, because of his faith and his trust and his hope, Jesus did cure his blindness. When questioned about it later, by the authorities, the man did not have a lengthy explanation. All he knew was that he was blind, and Jesus touched him, and now he could see. When something positive happens to you and you cannot explain it, remember this story. There may not be an explanation but you know it happened because it changed you.

# Ordinary People

HAVE YOU EVER stood in line at the checkout counter of the supermarket and perused the covers of magazines like PEOPLE and thought to yourself, "Wouldn't it be fun to be famous?" Think again. If you cherish the "beautiful people" magazines, then you are also subject to the hideous pictures and untrue stories of famous people in the tabloids and realize how fortunate you are to just be *ordinary*. You are free to go wherever you wish, associate with whomever you wish without flashbulbs snapping in your face when you are out with your family, or strangers stopping by your dinner table at restaurants, interrupting your meal and wanting an autograph. We don't have to be famous to spread God's love. In fact, it might be easier because we are *ordinary*.

Both the Old and New Testament give accounts of how God used *ordinary* people in mighty ways. Ruth was a young widow who loved and cared for her widowed mother-in-law, Naomi. There was no welfare plan then; no money to care for widows. They were living in a country called Moab. Naomi decided to return to her homeland, Bethlehem in Judah, where she had relatives. She advised Ruth to return to her family in Moab but Ruth chose to accompany Naomi to Bethlehem saying, *Ruth 1:16b,* ***"Your people shall be my people and your God my God."*** They returned to Bethlehem and Ruth provided their food, in a most humble way, by gleaning.

*Ruth 2: 2-4*: **And Ruth the Moabitess said to Naomi, "Let me go to the fields and pick up the leftover grain behind anyone in whose eyes I find favor." Naomi said to her, "Go ahead, my daughter," So she went out and began to glean in the fields behind the harvesters. As it turned out, she found herself working in a field belonging to Boaz, who was from the clan of Elimelech.** *Ordinary* Ruth eventually married Boaz and bore him a son who would become the grandfather of King David. Ruth did not know God used her to continue the line of David, eventually to Jesus. God uses *us* in powerful ways, also, whether we know it or not.

How did God choose the king of Israel? Did he look for someone prominent? Popular? No. He sent his servant, Samuel to the home of Jesse, who had several sons. God told Samuel that He was going to choose one of Jesse's sons to become the ruler of Israel. The first son had excellent attributes, to which Samuel said, "Surely this is the Lord's choice," but it was not God's choice, *1Samuel 16:7*: **But the Lord said to Samuel, "Do not consider his appearance or his height, for I have rejected him. The Lord does not look at the things man looks at. Man looks at the outward appearance, but the Lord looks at the heart."** None of the seven sons was God's choice. Samuel asked Jesse if he had any more sons and he replied, "Only my youngest son, David, who is tending the sheep. Samuel asked to see him and when David was brought before Samuel, God said this was his choice to rule Israel. A shepherd then was as ordinary as one is today and yet God chose David to become possibly the most important king of all time.

In the New Testament, we read about Mary, the mother of Jesus. She was in love with her fiancé, a carpenter. To people around her, she was an *ordinary* young woman but, to God,

Mary was so special, she would be loved and honored for time immortal.

When Jesus began His public ministry, who did He choose as followers to carry on His message of redemption? Read *Mark 1:16-17,* **As Jesus walked beside the Sea of Galilee, he saw Simon and his bother Andrew casting a net into the lake, for they were fishermen. "Come, follow me," Jesus said, "and I will make you fishers of men." At once they left their nets and followed him.** Did He choose wealthy land owners, political leaders, or charismatic public speakers? No. Jesus chose fishermen. Through twelve *ordinary* men, He developed a ministry that is still strong and powerful, 2,000+ years later.

Just as in biblical times, God chooses *ordinary* people in our lifetime to become powerful examples. Mother Theresa, a very common and ordinary nun devoted her life to the underprivileged in India. Billy Graham, an *ordinary* farm boy became a world famous evangelist. God also wants to empower you and me as we go about our *ordinary* daily routine. We may not even recognize when we reflect God's love by giving hope, courage, comfort or renewed faith to someone but it will happen.

Our young people can be very influential to their peers. A high school student named Jim totally cleaned out his locker one Friday. As he walked home, struggling to balance his books, another student, whom he recognized but didn't know, asked if he could help. "My name is Wayne," he introduced himself as he picked up the fallen books and walked along side Jim. They talked and got acquainted until they reached Jim's house and he thanked Wayne for the help. "No problem," replied Wayne. "I'll see you next week." This *ordinary* act of kindness was to change a student's life.

As Jim put things away, he thought about how nice it was of Wayne to help him. "Maybe the reason I don't have many friends is that I'm not very friendly," he thought. "I never speak first. If Wayne had not spoken first, I would have ignored him. Maybe I turn people off by ignoring them." On Monday, Jim went to school with a new attitude. Instead of walking around with his eyes on the floor, he looked up and greeted people and began finding ways, simple ways, to help others. He wanted to be more like Wayne.

The two boys graduated in the same class. Jim was valedictorian. In his speech, he didn't mention names but spoke of kindness and friendship. "If someone in this class had not shown me kindness last year, I might not be here. I would not have the many friends I have here today and I would not be valedictorian." He continued, "You see, last year I was very discouraged. Things were not going well at home or at school so, one Friday, I cleaned out my locker because I decided to commit suicide. Then, another student came along and helped me carry my stuff. We talked and, somehow, I felt better and I decided to try and find small ways to help others in the same way I had been helped. I made some friends and my work improved. I want to thank that classmate for giving me a reason to live."

When we serve others, even in the most quiet, personal, private ways, we are serving God. We are giving the word *ordinary* special meaning. A plaque hangs on the wall in my office that says, "**Success consists of doing the common things in life uncommonly well**." God knocks on the door of your heart and mind and intellect. He says, "I need *ordinary* you to do the common things in life uncommonly well as you serve *Me* by serving those around you.

# Pentecost

PENTECOST IS AN important day on the Church calendar because it reminds us of that moment in time when simple, ordinary men were given a special gift that would change the world. Fifty days had passed since that Passover supper when Jesus and the apostles gathered to celebrate and remember the miraculous release of their people by the Egyptians. Jesus tried to tell the apostles about his impending death and resurrection but they didn't understand until it was over and they *witnessed* the risen Christ.

Now, they met for another special meal. These were not just random get-togethers. They were commands from God to Moses for the Israelites after their release from Egypt. They were told that their generation, and all future Jewish generations, were to celebrate certain occasions at certain times. The apostles gathered together to remember Pentecost, a time of thanksgiving and sacrifice to God for the bounty of their first fruits after arriving in the Promised Land. Suddenly, the sound of a gale force wind filled the room and what appeared like tongues of fire settled on their heads and they began speaking in languages other than their own. The Bible tells us that the Holy Spirit was giving them this ability.

Godly Jews from many lands, who were in town for the religious celebration, heard the apostles speaking and recognized them as ordinary people with no special training. Yet, they were speaking in *their* native languages; not bumbling through or with a few chosen words as a tourist might speak but, as the Bible says, "in their mother tongue." In other words, perfect language as one is taught from birth. This is not something the apostles knew was coming or asked for. It was God's plan to spread the Gospel to many nations quickly; to ignite the flame that caused a wild fire that could not be contained. It continues today throughout the world. It must have been a huge surprise to the relatively uneducated apostles and yet they probably were thrilled to have this special ability to tell others about God's amazing love. When the visitors heard God's message, and reported it back to their countrymen, they were probably much more believable than the apostles, had they been able to go to all these countries as missionaries.

I was once involved with a program that brought the Gospel to countries not allowing foreign missionaries. Strong believers, who had good positions or authority in those countries, were sent to Singapore where they studied how to share the Gospel and brought the message of salvation back to their country-men. They were much more accepted and believed than a well meaning foreigner missionary who could not even speak their language. I believe that what happened on Pentecost had the same affect.

Speaking a different language spontaneously isn't common today, but there are those who ask for, and are given the gift of tongues within a religious context and they have a special prayer language. Then, there are other circumstances that involve a new language.

When I worked as an activity director in a nursing home, one of our elderly residents named Elsie had a stroke that left her in a coma for a few days. After she revived, it appeared that her speech was impaired and limited to a few sounds. She would sit in her wheelchair by the window, point outside, and mumble some noises. The Staff and her family all agreed that she must be very confused until a visitor came in one day to see a friend. Elsie was sitting near them, quietly mumbling and pointing out the window. The visitor listened carefully and when a Staff member said she hoped Elsie was not interfering with their conversation, the visitor said, "Not at all. She's speaking Old German. It's very garbled but I understand it perfectly," and the visitor spoke a few words back. Elsie pointed to the window and the visitor said, "She's telling us about the sun." Elsie's family was dumbfounded because no language other than English had ever been spoken in their house. They learned that friends and relatives from the old country spoke Old German in Elsie's home when she was very young and hearing others was her only exposure to the language.

Elsie's experience has no comparison to the profoundness of the apostles' experience. Skeptics ridiculed the apostles and accused them of being drunk because they didn't believe there was any way that ordinary people could suddenly speak another language. This example shows that it can happen, even in today's world. None of our Staff understood her mumbling so we thought she was confused or disoriented until someone who spoke the native language interpreted what she was saying. We may not experience something as dramatic as the apostles but, as Christians, we are all gifted by God through the Holy Spirit and that makes us who we are and allows us to impact our world and affect those around us.

We do nothing out-of-the ordinary, but God uses us. I fostered many children over a period of years and considered it nothing more than our way of life. I cannot remember one time when I felt out-of-the-ordinary or thought I was using some special gift but realize now that just plain ordinary mothering was a gift and whatever I did was with God's direction.

The apostles did not ask for and were not expecting anything unusual to affect their lives but God needed them to carry His message of redemption and hope to people in far-away places where the apostles would never go. So, God gave them the ability to speak different languages in order to attract people from far-away places who would take the message back to their countrymen. The Bible tells us that these visiting Jews were so impressed by this happening that 3,000 were baptized and became believers that day and many more followed in days to come. It would have been impossible for the apostles to reach this many people in such a powerful way if God had not gifted them. God wants to gift you and me with abilities to make our days here on earth count for Him as we go about our ordinary routine. Make yourself available and He will make the time count.

# Gardens

MEET ME IN the garden. For me, there are two important gardens in the Bible; Eden and Gethsemane. Let's go to the Garden of Eden. *Genesis 2:8-10a*: **Now the Lord God had planted a garden in the east, in Eden; and there he put the man he had formed. And the Lord God made all kinds of trees grow out of the ground --- trees that were pleasing to the eye and good for food. In the middle of the garden were the tree of life and the tree of the knowledge of good and evil. A river watering the garden flowed from Eden.** The Bible doesn't really tell us a lot about this garden except that it was perfect; a perfect gift to Adam and Eve. It provided gorgeous scenery, good food and, for a while, every day was a perfect day.

Have you ever experienced a perfect day? They are few and far between. Something unexpected happens; someone you love speaks unkindly to you, it rains on your outdoor event, the car battery is dead and you are already late for an appointment. What happened to the perfect day? Perfection is not part of our daily life and hasn't been since the *Garden*. Temptation took over and God's will for His people was replaced by disobedience.

Perhaps we still have a *Garden of Eden* attitude, not too different from Adam and Eve. God provides for us abundantly. Our pantry, refrigerator, garage and closet are full, or at least we have more than most of us need to survive. God provides and asks very little of us in return. He says, "Share." He says, "Be nice." He says, "Honor Me with your words." He says, "Be honest," and we disobey and our garden - our perfect world becomes overrun with weeds and we are caught in creeping vines. Life is not as easy as we hoped, as easy as it could have been if we had a desire to obey and please God.

Meet me at the Red Sea. The Israelites had been freed from slavery and Moses was leading them across the desert. The king of Egypt sent hundreds of chariots to chase after and defeat them. They were gaining ground and the Israelites were frightened. *Exodus 14:13-14:* **And Moses said to the people, "Do not be afraid. Stand still, and see the salvation of the Lord, which He will accomplish for you today. For the Egyptians whom you see today, you shall see again no more forever."** And, so it was; the Israelites crossed on dry land and the Egyptians were swallowed up by the sea and killed. God performed the impossible for the Israelites and He can do the same for you and me.

When my husband and I were fostering children, two little sisters came to live with us while they waited to be adopted into a suitable family. The three year old was a chubby little blue eyed blonde with a ready smile and a sweet disposition. Her five year old sister was malnourished with skinny legs like a bird and she was a mean little kid. She had every right to be. She had cigarette burn scars on her chest and back and needle marks in her arms where we suspect her mother shot her up with heroin. She was so traumatized, she could not talk and took her feelings out on the innocent three year old who apparently was never physically mistreated in their home. The older child constantly taunted the younger one and made her little life miserable. I would lie awake nights thinking of ways to keep them separated, worrying about them in their new adoptive home. In my mind, they were symbolically at the Red Sea of their lives with no possible way to get to the other side. But, God had a plan and used some very wise social workers to help execute it. They adopted out the girls separately; something I never thought of. The little one went to an energetic young couple and the older one was adopted by an older couple who had already put into place a plan that included counseling and special tutoring. They were taking on a gigantic challenge but it was probably the best possible opportunity for this angry, very abused and hurt little girl to find some peace and normalcy in her life. Symbolically, God parted their Red Sea and they passed over on dry ground, each to their own *promised land*. I watched a modern exodus.

Meet me at the other garden; the garden of Gethsemane. The garden of olive trees, also called the Mount of Olives. *Luke 22:41-44:* **He withdrew about a stone's throw beyond them, knelt down and prayed, "Father, if you are willing, take this cup from me; yet not my will, but yours be done." An angel from heaven appeared to him and strengthened him. And being in anguish, he prayed more earnestly, and his sweat was like drops of blood falling to the ground.** Jesus was humanly overcome with sorrow because of what was ahead for Him. He knew the pain and agony that was unavoidable if He was to accomplish his mission here on earth.

Most of us have had moments of hopeless agony when we threw ourselves on the mercy of God and prayed that something unavoidable could be changed whether it regarded prison or illness or possible death. Jesus knows your experience because He had something even worse. Your experience involves *you* or someone you love. His experience involved the entire human race. Don't feel that you are hopelessly, helplessly being dragged down uncharted waters in a boat without oars; headed for some dark abyss because you feel out of control over what is happening to you or someone you love. Jesus says, "I've been there. I know. Trust me."

Our last meeting is the most important of all. Meet me at the cross. *Luke 23:39-43*: **One of the criminals who hung there hurled insults at him: "Aren't you the Christ? Save yourself and us:" But the other criminal rebuked him. "Don't you fear God,"** **he said, "since you are under the same sentence? We are punished justly, for we are getting what our deeds deserve. But this man has done nothing wrong." Then, he said, "Jesus, remember me when you come into your kingdom." Jesus answered him, "I tell you the truth, today you will be with me in paradise."** Crowds of people shouted their demand that Jesus die on the cross. A passerby was made to carry the cross when Jesus became too weak. Women followers of Jesus stood apart from Him and cried. Priests, people in high places and soldiers made fun of Jesus. They hurled insults at Him, as did one of the two criminals also being crucified.

Where do *you* fit into this picture? Would you be one to cry "Crucify Him!" because you wanted to be part of the crowd and not make waves by opposing the masses? Would you carry the cross because you were made to do it? Would you weep in the background? Would you hurl insults at Jesus? Or, would you recognize who he really was and ask to be remembered in His kingdom? I know where I *hope* I would be but it scares me to wonder how I might have acted then. Think about it. The important thing to remember is that Jesus *chose* to die this death, so painful and horrendous, that at one point he felt separated from God when he cried out, *"My God, why have you forsaken me?"* Jesus chose this one experience in the history of mankind because He was in love..........................

> >
> >
> >
> >
> >
> >
> >
> >

with *YOU!!!*

# Psalm 23

**THE LORD IS my shepherd, I shall not want.**

Sheep are not considered the smartest animals in the world and they are especially confused and easily lost when left alone. They wander aimlessly and are easy prey for predators. However, under the leadership of a good shepherd, they are herded into groups where they feel safe and content. Their needs are filled. They do not want for anything. They trust their shepherd to lead them safely to their final destination.

You and I are like the sheep that wander aimlessly, easy prey for predators that recognize us when we are at our lowest ebb. They lure us by pretending to be our friends when, in reality, they desire to prey on our weaknesses for their own gain. When our children are bored and seeking excitement or escaping what they consider a difficult home life, Satan uses someone to lure them and they can spend the rest of their lives differently than they had planned. Drugs and excess alcohol can weaken the brain and body to where they will never be as sharp again. Nothing will be the same when we choose to be lured away by momentary pleasures and wander beyond the safety of our shepherd.

With the Lord as our shepherd, we have a leader who does not want us to wander through life aimlessly and alone. In His care, we sense that we are safe and feel content. He knows our needs even before we ask. We choose not to wander away when our mind is clear and our good judgment tells us that we are making wise choices.

*He makes me lie down in green pastures. He leads me beside quiet waters. He restores my soul.*

When evening comes, the shepherd doesn't bed his flock down on dry weeds and painful thistles. He looks for soft, fresh grass that fills the need for both comfort and food. The nearby water is quiet and safe to walk into or drink. The sheep are totally refreshed and at peace for the night. Are you at peace when you bed down for the night?

If we stray from His guidance, then we begin to encounter unfamiliar surroundings that make us feel lost. The familiar landmarks have disappeared. The lush pasture becomes a swamp of temptation. Just as it doesn't take long for a wandering sheep to leave the flock and run in the wrong direction, so it is with us when we wander from God's will. We quickly get sucked in by the predators of worldly delights. Then we sink into mire that is a struggle to escape from.

Each of us knows what tempts us most. We need to be very aware so we don't get caught in the quicksand of sin. It is so easy to step into and almost impossible to pull ourselves out. In fact, sometimes the wicked draw of Satan is beyond our humanness and only intervention by a loving, *forgiving* God can save us. That restores our soul.

*He guides me in paths of righteousness for his name's sake.*

The shepherd leads his flock in the right direction so no harm comes to them. God leads us in the right direction for the same reason.

*Even though I walk through the valley of the shadow of death, I will fear no evil for you are with me.*

No matter how good the shepherd is, sometimes it is

necessary to travel a rough, possibly dangerous path in order to reach the final destination of rich, green pasture. The risk of predators is very real. The terrain is dangerous with steep gorges that surely would kill or severely injure the sheep if they fell. Yet, they are not afraid because their shepherd is dependable; always keeping them close to each other and close to him.

Our Good Shepherd protects us from danger by telling us to stay close to Him. How do we do this? First, by believing He is real and then by recognizing that He has provided good advice for us in the Bible, and then by understanding that we have direct communication with Him in prayer. Even when we are in physical danger, almost to the point of death, or spiritual danger when *something* or *someone* tries to draw us away from God, He reminds us to remain close to Him where He can protect us from the gravest dangers.

If we *choose* to break away and follow another path and we do this over and over, refusing to listen to our shepherd, we set ourselves up for failure. We do not answer when He repeatedly calls our name. We choose to risk never being able to return to the safety of His flock. We *choose* to be lost. Whatever our weakness; alcohol, drugs, gambling, pornography or some other magnetic draw, everyone close to us is affected and hurt. Many times their lives are changed, too. That is *not* God's plan for us.

**Your rod and your staff, they comfort me.**

Only a shepherd truly understands the importance of the rod and staff. They are the best "tools of the trade" because they keep the sheep within his control. The shepherd herds the lead sheep with his rod and the flock follows. Should one stray and fall into a crevice or somehow get out of reach, the shepherd comes to the rescue with the crook of his staff, hooking it around the fallen sheep and pulling it up and out of danger. The rod is a tool that wards off predators before they can do harm to the flock. Good advice from the Bible is symbolic of God's rod and staff that protect us from dangerous influences and rescue us from possible harm.

*You prepare a table before me in the presence of my enemies.*

Who or what are your enemies? Are they people who lure you away from God in your weakness? Is your enemy a disease; Cancer, Parkinson's, Diabetes? Is it alcohol, drugs, some other physical or mental or spiritual foe? Is your enemy fear of death or fear of life? After my husband died, my enemy was grief. It tried to consume me and I worked hard to stay ahead of it and not get drawn into the quicksand of its pull. God tells us that, if we trust Him, He will honor us before our very *enemies* until our cup of joy and peace absolutely fills to overflowing. He is more powerful, beyond our human understanding, than any enemy that tries to attack us.

*You anoint my head with oil. My cup overflows.*

When I look at the beauty of the earth around us, my cup overflows. When I receive a telephone call from one of our children, checking in to make sure I'm OK, my cup overflows. When I think of friends who show love toward me in so many ways, my cup overflows.

*Surely, goodness and mercy will follow me all the days of my life and I will live in the house of the Lord forever.*

Life on earth will never be perfect but it can come close when we remember that this is only the beginning. Eternal life with God promises to be perfect and worth the wait. In the meantime, depend on goodness and mercy to dwell with you and bring you personal peace that comes with following the good shepherd.

# Windfalls

SOMETHING DIFFERENT CAME in the mail recently and immediately caught my attention because the envelope was fat and
full and from a group of attorneys in southern Minnesota (where
my father said that even the roosters crowed in Norwegian). I
was more curious than concerned because I could think of no
reason for an attorney to contact me. The papers told in usual
legal jargon that a man, whom I never heard of but who had the
same last name as my Mother's maiden name, had died and it
gave a brief overview of his will. He had no living parents, sib-
lings or children but he did have a slew of distant cousins and
my name was among them.

He left an estate of several thousand dollars and I must admit that, as I read on, my heart skipped a beat or two. A portion
went to the church and a couple of veteran's organizations but
the bulk of the estate was willed to a long time friend who had
not only shared this cousin's healthy years but willingly cared
for him through a lengthy illness prior to death. The friend expected nothing more than companionship but was the recipient
of a windfall. The reason cousins were notified was to acknowledge that none of us was mentioned in the will; probably a way
of avoiding anyone contesting it.

The dictionary expresses windfalls as *sudden or unexpected
gains*. Some windfalls are blatantly apparent and others can be

subtle until we give them some thought and realize how fortunate we are.

A blatant windfall was experienced by Joseph as related in Genesis. He was the spoiled youngest son of Jacob. At least his brothers considered him as spoiled since Jacob favored Joseph and made him the coat of many colors. Joseph also had the gift of interpreting dreams, which the brothers resented and, while they were all out grazing the flock, they plotted to kill Joseph. Instead, they sold him to a passing tribe who made him their slave. He was seventeen years old. The brothers dipped the coat of many colors in the blood of a goat they slaughtered and brought it back to their father saying Joseph must have been killed by a wild animal.

Joseph lived in slavery in Egypt and was eventually accused falsely of an act he did not commit and was placed in a dungeon. Life could not have taken a worse turn when, at the age of thirty, everything changed because of Joseph's ability to interpret dreams. Through all the indignities he had suffered, Joseph remained true to his faith and God blessed him with this unique ability. The Pharaoh had some disturbing dreams that only Joseph could interpret. They had to do with the survival of Egypt during a horrendous famine.

*Genesis 41* tells a thrilling story of how Joseph gained the Pharaoh's favor and became second in command of all Egypt. Joseph was the recipient of an amazing windfall, a sudden and unexpected gain.

In the gospels, we read of two criminals who were crucified along with Jesus. One insulted Jesus but the other one rebuked the insulter. Read *Luke 23:39-43*. He asked Jesus for forgiveness. He received the most remarkable windfall, a sudden and unexpected gain, when Jesus invited him into His kingdom that very day.

Windfalls also happen in our time. One of the most profound inheritances that people in my generation received was the GI Bill after WWII. Inherited from our imaginary Uncle Sam, veterans were given the privilege of a college education in appreciation of their military service to our country. It not only changed the life of the recipient, the trickle-down effect changed our entire society as men and women graduated from colleges they could never have afforded to attend on their own and went on to achieve success beyond their fondest dreams. The masses were being highly educated and these expanded minds catapulted our society and our world into previously unimaginable modernization.

Science, farming, industry, medicine and trade flourished. Many of us are alive today who would not have survived fifty years ago. Illness and disease can be treated and cured now because of research and development that was never available to us then. Returning veterans had the opportunity and privilege to attend medical school.

Farming has become a science in the hands of creative inventors of new techniques and equipment. The computer, microwave, cell phone and literally thousands of other items that make life easier and more affordable to the masses were invented by men and women who entered the armed forces with no motive or goal beyond protecting our country from the ravages of WWII. As recipients of a windfall, they changed the world.

For me, the most important sudden and unexpected gain has to be salvation. Jesus didn't wait for us to change our life style, clean up our act, abandon our habits or addictions, be nicer or try harder. He didn't wait until we promised to be better. I paraphrase *Romans 5:6*, ***While we were just like we are right now, helpless and hopeless, Christ died for us***. Is there any windfall that is more powerful? When we least expected it or least deserved it, Christ died for us.

I think back to the letter I received from the lawyers that said someone died and I didn't get anything. That was OK because I knew I didn't deserve anything. I'm so glad I didn't get a letter from God saying, "My son died but you don't get anything because you don't deserve it." Instead I have a letter in the Bible that says, "Jesus died for you and left you a promised inheritance -- eternal life with Him."

# Another Burp

ONE DAY, THE pastor visited me at my home. He mentioned that there would be a conference in San Diego and it was important that someone represent our church. I didn't know where this conversation was leading but, since I wasn't sure what the pastor was talking about and, obviously, had never attended such a gathering, I kept my mouth shut. He finally got around to the punch line. "I was wondering if you might be interested in this event?" He went on to say the expenses would be paid and I was expected to take notes and report back to the congregation.

I thanked the pastor for his confidence in me but told him I did not know anything about church politics and I was sure someone with a lot more experience than me would do a better job. He looked disappointed. Finally, I said, "I tell you what. Please ask every possible person in the church first and, if they all decline, then ask me."

He replied, "I already did."

# The Weakest Link

HAVE YOU EVER belonged to a group of people you thoroughly enjoyed; people you were comfortable with, possibly people you have known for some time? What happens when someone new joins such a group? This might be a new member of your family, new co-worker, new student at school or a neighbor who joins your study group or club. Even when there is no apparent reason for it, a new person in a solid, stable group can be a temporary threat. The new person becomes the weakest link in our once comfortably strong chain. Let me tell you a success story about some young women I knew.

Several years ago, I happened to see a friend of my oldest daughter in the supermarket. I had once led a Bible Study for a group of these young women when they were about eighteen years old. After a couple years, some of them went away to school, a few got married, and the group disbanded so it was a delight to once again see this friend who now had two preschoolers in the shopping cart. She told me that some of the women from the former Bible Study, and a few new ones, would like to start another one and relate it to their present circumstance of marriage and parenthood. Would I lead it? I agreed and told her the days that were best for me. A few days later she called to say the study would be held on Tuesday mornings from nine to eleven at the home of one of the mothers and there was a room where the children could be tended by a baby sitter they would hire.

While these plans were in the making, I became aware of a young couple who lived in an older trailer on the property of the fire station where I volunteered on the Rescue Squad. Bob and Kim married shortly after high school graduation and now, four years later, were the parents of three preschoolers with another baby on the way. Bob was a part time fire fighter and I knew their income was low. To my knowledge, they had few friends and no social life beyond the fire station. They appeared to have no relationship with the Lord and did not attend any church. One night after Rescue Squad training, I paid them a visit, not knowing what kind of a reception I would get. I told Kim about the Bible Study for mothers of preschoolers that was about to begin and she and Bob both seemed open to the idea. He even encouraged her to go so she accepted and I wrote down the address where we were to meet. On the appointed day, Kim pulled into the driveway right behind me in her very old, unreliable, station wagon. The hostess' husband was a young attorney and the house was a large Mediterranean style with more than enough room for Bible Study and child care.

Most of the nine women there knew each other but there were a few strangers like Kim, although I assumed from their designer jeans that they were in a very different income bracket than she. Without a doubt, Kim was to be our weakest link. 1 Cor. 12:22, **and some of the parts that seem weakest and least important are really the most necessary.** We had a brief social time with coffee and settled down to a Bible Study followed by discussion of what they hoped to learn from the Word. I also asked what areas of their personal life they wanted to share or change.

I gave Kim a Living Bible but she didn't have a clue how

to use it. The gal next to her helped her out and she seemed comfortable with that. The Bible wasn't the only thing she didn't know about. In the discussion that followed, she told us she didn't know how to cook. Her father did the cooking in the home where she was raised and she was trying to learn but struggling. Just the night before, her husband complained about the spaghetti so she took the serving bowl, sauce and all, and dumped it upside down over his head. This was our introduction to Kim. I sat back and watched the other girls interact with her, wondering if they would chide or belittle her. To my delight, they felt some connection with what she was going through and, after a few nervous remarks; they gave her some suggestions about spaghetti and promised a few easy recipes the following week. *Ephesians 4:2,* ***Be humble and gentle. Be patient with each other, making allowance for each other's faults because of your love.***

One of the gals gave Kim her phone number and encouraged a call if she had any questions before the next lesson. As the weeks progressed, Kim was determined to learn how to use the Bible. Many of these girls went to the same church and made occasional invitations to Kim but there was no pressure and Kim never went. After the study time, the girls shared prayer concerns and we all wrote them down, promising to put them in some conspicuous place so we would be reminded daily to pray. It was apparent that each of these young women had concerns for their families, marriage, relationships, and health. A good education and good salary did not shield them from life's challenges.

Some of these women were very discouraged. Kim was not discouraged but she was overwhelmed with the responsibility of parenthood and her ignorance about so many things. She also shared that she had little support. Her husband tried but was almost as ignorant about parenting as she and his family openly displayed their dislike for her. Her own family was apathetic and she had few friends her age. The Bible Study group became her best friends although she did not see them between meetings. Still, she felt a kinship that was a new experience and there was a love of friends that seemed unconditional and sincere. *Galatians 6:10,* ***That's why, whenever we can, we should always be kind to everyone and especially to our Christian brothers and sisters.***

After several weeks of perfect attendance, Kim didn't show up. We called her but got no answer so we began the study without her. At 10:30, someone glanced out the window and spotted Kim walking down the street (there were no sidewalks) pushing two children in an old stroller and carrying the youngest, propped up on her pregnant tummy. It had taken her almost two hours because one of the wheels kept falling off the stroller. She was hot and sweaty but determined to make it to Bible Study and told us the station wagon broke down the night before. Something else she shared for the first time was that she had a job cleaning stalls at a nearby stable. Each morning she spent two hours shoveling manure, sweeping stalls and placing clean straw down. It was early while her husband and children were still asleep. This morning, she rose at 3:30 AM in order to walk to and from the stable, get home in time to dress the children and walk to Bible Study. We stayed around longer that day. Someone drove Kim and her children home. Not all the other girls were financially secure but all of them were much better off than Kim. Yet, she taught them something profound that day about commitment, desire and perseverance. Our weakest link was beginning to show us her strength. Psalms 34:1-3, ***I will praise the Lord no matter what happens. I will constantly speak of His glories and*** *grace. I will boast of all His kindness to me. Let all who are discouraged take heart. Let us praise the Lord together and exalt His name.*

Where it once seemed quite one-sided, that Kim was on the receiving end of suggestions and advice, some of the young mothers were now looking to her for ideas because she was so practical. When they complained about the time it took to transport their children to a swimming pool and wait hours for them to play and cool off, or when they complained about the cost of water toys and how they would break, it was Kim who suggested they purchase a cheap paint brush for each child, give them a pan of water outside and let them paint the house and the car and each other which kept them busy for hours in their own back yard.

At one meeting, a mother complained that their family did very little together and some of the other mothers agreed. The husbands were busy day and night building their fortunes. 1 Tim. 6:6-7: *Do you want to be truly rich? You already are if you are happy and good. After all, we didn't bring any money with us when we came into the world and we can't carry away a single penny when we die.* The husbands attended church but that wasn't quality *communicating* time with their families. The women were lonely in their big, expensive homes. Kim suggested they choose different names from a hat every couple weeks and call that person just to keep in touch and share any concerns. In doing so, they became much better acquainted. Those who picked Kim's name found her to be a real encourager. *Proverbs 12:25,* **Anxious hearts are very heavy but a word of encouragement does wonders.**

Although the girls found new companionship with each other, they still wanted some quality time with their families so I suggested they talk with their husbands and, together, create a new tradition that could be accomplished each week. They were to bring their suggestions back to Bible Study and every one of them brought back a different idea. One couple took their children to the donut shop on Saturday mornings and another went miniature golfing. Kim and Bob took their children for a walk, each week in a different direction. The cost was zero and the dividends were enormous.

Several months went by since we began Bible Study and summer was approaching. Kim had a successful delivery of her new baby and enjoyed the comfort and attention from her Bible Study friends. Most of the mothers were involved in planning Bible School at their Church. They encouraged Kim to come along and bring her children who now knew many other children from Bible Study. She accepted the invitation and helped where she could. Before long, Kim was a regular at the Sunday service and was baptized. Now, she had more than a group of friends. She became part of the family of God. Bob began attending family gatherings at the church and eventually studied with the pastor for membership. About a year later he also accepted Christ and was baptized.

This all began with the desire of a few young mothers to meet and learn about God's will for them from studying the Bible and supporting each other in fellowship and prayer. It was a successful experience because they accepted each other unconditionally and encouraged each other and learned from each other. It was successful because they did not allow the weak link to remain weak but strengthened her wherever they could and recognized where she strengthened them until, eventually, all the links in the chain were strong and supportive.

2 Cor. 1:3-4, *What a wonderful God we have – He is the father of our Lord Jesus Christ, the source of every mercy and*

*the one who so wonderfully comforts and strengthens us in our hardships and trials. And why does He do this? So that when others are troubled, needing our sympathy and encouragement, we can pass on to them this same help and comfort God has given us.*

# Freedom

JULY 4, is very important to every American. We celebrate the moment in history when our countrymen declared independence from Britain. We commemorate the adoption of the Declaration of Independence in 1776, and the birth of our democracy.

Freedom is never free. The struggle for freedom usually involves conflict or war and the result includes loss of life. Young people you and I never met sacrifice their lives for us. Until we know someone who died in service to our country, it is difficult to comprehend that *they are no longer here so we can be.* When we realize their cost for our freedom, we cannot help but be brought to our knees in thanksgiving for this blessed gift of life at someone else's expense.

Freedom doesn't always involve war. It can involve enslavement. The Israelites were enslaved by the Egyptians for hundreds of years. Moses implored the Egyptian leader to, "Let my people go." His plea fell on deaf ears and God finally intervened and caused plagues and great hardship to come upon the Egyptians, culminating in the death of every family's first born son and the first born of their animals. Then Pharaoh, Egypt's leader, told the Israelites to leave quickly and they did. The number was about 600,000 men plus the women and children. After hundreds of years under the whip of slave drivers, they now had their freedom.

Until about 1865, we had slaves here in America. About fifteen million slaves were brought to the Americas from Africa. They were packed into ships so tightly, chained together by hands and feet, that they could hardly move and many died on the voyage over. The survivors endured great hardship until they were freed at the end of the Civil War.

In our own time, some of us have seen freedom come to people who were prisoners in their own country. In 1961, a wall was erected that divided East Germany, controlled by the Communists and West Germany, controlled by their own free sovereign nation. Families were separated and jobs lost because travel back and forth was no longer permitted. Many people died in escape attempts from East to West Germany. President Reagan implored the leader of the Soviet Union saying, "Mr. Gorbachev, tear this wall down," and that is exactly what happened in 1989. We watched it on television as ecstatic family members were reunited when those in East Germany were set free to mingle with their family members and countrymen in West Germany. Freedom from tyranny is the same, whether for the Israelites, the Africans, the Germans or in the Middle East; whether it happened a few thousand years ago, a few hundred years ago or recently.

Freedom doesn't have to involve a race or nation or even a group of people. There are freedoms that can only be enjoyed by the individual. Living in the United States affords us special freedom because the entire country belongs to its citizens who can go anywhere in the country without a passport or special permission. We are not confined to one state but are free to move about, visit, work or study.

In 1980, I was fortunate enough to accompany a group of college students to a communist country. The minute we arrived, we were assigned a guide who did not leave us for the entire trip. We were not allowed to wander away on our own or leave our lodging at night. Once, I tried to go a different direction from our group when we were being taken to a department store in a city and I had no interest in shopping. When our bus came to a stop, our instructions were to turn to the right as we exited the bus and I turned left instead and walked about a block. In that time, many local people tried to speak to me. Bicyclers stopped to greet me, practicing their limited English. Then, the whistles blew and police were all around me and I was cordially escorted back to where I belonged. The local people there were not allowed to gather in a group or stop and try to speak to me. My fellow travelers were taken to a department store where our American money was exchanged for play money that we could then use to purchase goods. This prohibited the locals from making any purchases because they did not have the play money.

Our guide had only one shirt, which he washed by hand every night. We asked him how he became a guide. Did he study for it? Was it the job he had always wanted? He said it was the job he was assigned for life and he had no choice to do something else. When our trip ended, we crossed the border by train. At the border were giant rolls of barbed wire with jagged glass at the top, creating an impossible escape. Everyone was unusually quiet while we passed by this symbol of enforced captivity. Once the giant rolls of barbed wire were behind us, and we knew we were no longer under the control of communism, the entire car erupted into cheers of relief. *We were free!*

Freedom also includes personal experiences. Medical science offers this freedom through organ transplants. If you are a willing organ donor when you die, I understand that many people can be helped from just one healthy donor. Think of it; patients who would otherwise die, or possibly be severely handicapped, are given a second chance at a better life, or life itself, through your generous gift.

The grandson of some friends was killed by a hit-run driver in early March one year as he walked his date home on the campus of the University of Oregon. He had just renewed his driver's license and told his mom that he was an organ donor. His parents honored this wish and had the doctors harvest as many organs as were not damaged by the accident. His heart went to a twenty-two year old young man from Florida. The surgery was a success but, as the man prepared to leave the hospital, he had a stroke and died. The doctors quickly re-harvested the healthy heart and placed it in the body of a ten year old boy who would have soon died without it. Because the young man who was killed had been in such good physical condition, many of his organs were appropriate for donation. The harvested lungs were given to a cystic fibrosis patient in Washington State. Imagine the freedom of a clean breath of air for the first time in your life.

Freedom comes in a variety of shapes and sizes. As a cancer survivor, I can tell you that the very word, *cancer*, was a death sentence at first. It was like being imprisoned without a trial for something I had not done. Then I had some tests and a doctor released me from my hopelessness by saying there were possibilities for recovery and cure. Freedom from any illness or pain is priceless.

None of the freedoms I mentioned come close to the freedom God assures us of when we trust our life to Jesus Christ; and invite Him to forgive our offenses and lead us through the good and bad that each day brings. Not only are we free from past guilt or disappointment or offense to others, we are no longer alone as we struggle through life. Jesus promised us a "comforter," the Holy Spirit, a constant companion who will never leave us. *John 14:25-27,* **All this I have spoken while still with you. But the Counselor, the Holy Spirit, whom the Father will send in my name, will teach you all the things and will remind you of everything I have said to you. Peace I leave with you; my peace I give you. I do not give to you as the world gives. Do not let your hearts be troubled and do not be afraid.**

Recently, I was invited by the chaplain at a juvenile correction facility to visit with three girls on a Saturday afternoon. The chaplain said they had a few questions about God. I naively drove out there with no concept of what they wanted to ask. These girls were all seventeen years old and incarcerated for a variety of crimes. Mostly, they were involved with drugs or gangs and were hardened by fear and survival tactics that got them into trouble. They were all sorry for the pain they caused their families and wanted to change so that when they left the Center they could be different people. Going back to their families meant going back to their old friends and neighborhood. It wasn't going to be easy to seek new friendships and a different way of life. Gang life was a way of "belonging" but it came at a high cost. They had to either stab someone or get beaten close to death, themselves, by other gang members. The only way out of the gang was, again, to be beaten severely by other gang members and this is what they faced upon returning to their old neighborhood and old environment.

I told them that I understood they had some questions about God and didn't know if I had the answers but would try. They began firing questions at me like bullets. *If God created the heavens and the earth, who created God? Where did God come from? Who is God? What is God? If you commit suicide, do you go to hell? What is hell? Where is hell? What is heaven?*

*Where is heaven? Will we know each other in heaven? How do you know?* Questions like this flowed out of them and I didn't know one answer. I did tell them that there was no doubt in my mind about a special freedom that is theirs for the asking. One of the girls said, "Free? While we are in here?" I told her, "yes" and explained that there are hardened criminals in prison who will never be released because of their crime but they have a freedom that can only come from an understanding about God and how He arranged for their total forgiveness through Christ. I told them what it says in *Romans 8:1-2,* **There is therefore now no condemnation to those who are in Christ Jesus, who do not walk according to the flesh but according to the Spirit. For the law of the Spirit of life in Christ Jesus has made me free from the law of sin and death.** I shared how faith in that truth exonerates them from their past and gives them the opportunity to start life with a clean slate. We talked about how they could return home to old neighborhoods and old gangs and have the power to rise above the influence they no longer saw as something they admired and wanted to emulate.

Have you ever felt trapped? Maybe you were in jail or prison. Maybe you were a slave to alcohol or drugs or some other powerful habit. Maybe you hated your job but saw no way out or your relationship with another person was falling apart. And then, you were released from jail or prison. Do you remember that freedom? Or you kicked that habit and realized you had *power*. Do you remember that freedom? Or you learned a different skill that allowed you to change jobs. Remember that freedom? Perhaps you received some counseling that allowed you to make brave decisions about your relationship. Remember that freedom?

As we celebrate the freedoms that we enjoy in this wonderful country, and remember the sacrifices others made for us, not just in our lifetime but throughout the ages, let us be especially mindful of God's love and Christ's ultimate sacrifice for us. Whoever we are, whatever we have done, the slate is wiped clean and we are free for the asking if we are willing to accept changes and move in a new direction, following God's lead.

# Been There, Done That

EACH OF US represents a collage of experiences, good and bad. When we share the good, something happy or exciting or personally satisfying, we generally feel that the people listening to us can relate. They know happy. They know exciting. They know satisfying. However, when we have what we consider a bad experience, a loss; not just a loss to death but the loss of a friendship, a job, a body part to surgery, or having to move, we hesitate sharing our true feelings because we assume that no one will really understand.

A Hospice nurse and I facilitated Grief Recovery classes at our church in Northern California. These classes were open to the community and attracted people from all over Sacramento and surrounding areas. The series lasted six weeks. Before the first class of one of the sessions, a gentleman approached me to say that his name was Frank and he had recently lost his wife of forty-five years. "I know these other people had serious losses also," he said, "but there is no loss like the loss of one's wife."

After the participants had been seated in a circle, we asked each one to relate to the group who they lost and circumstances surrounding the experience. The thirty-one year old woman on one side of Frank told about her young husband who was killed on a business trip to Seattle while riding in a car driven by a drunk driver. She not only lost her husband but the father of her three young children, ages eight, five and three. She now faced the very real possibility of losing her house with its possessions and her car, besides having to seek employment and find affordable child care. On the other side of Frank sat a grandmother who, with her husband, took their four year old grandson to the ocean to play in the shallow water's edge. While they watched him from only 20 feet away, a huge wave covered him and an undertow sucked him out to sea, never to be seen again. Others in the circle of strangers had gathered to try to make some sense of the death of their loved one and the unbearable pain each one felt. The statement Frank made could have been made by any one of them. They each felt alone in their experience and their only commonality was the pain of their loss.

Although it accompanies the pain of a loved one's death, loneliness can happen anywhere, from work to school to church to home. It is hard to explain, let alone expect someone else to understand. *Mark 6: 1-4* tells us, **Jesus left there and went to his hometown, accompanied by his disciples. And when the Sabbath came, he began to teach in the synagogue. And many who heard him were amazed. "Where did this man get these things?" they asked. "What's this wisdom that has been given him, that he even does miracles! Isn't this the carpenter? Isn't this Mary's son and brother of James, Joseph, Judas, and Simon? Aren't his sisters here with us?" And they took offence at him. Jesus said to them, "Only in his hometown, among his relatives and in his own house is a prophet without honor."**

Jesus had lived most of his thirty years in Nazareth. He must have known many people on a first name basis as they watched him grow from childhood to adulthood. Probably he worked for some of them as a carpenter. Yet, Jesus was not welcome in his own town by people who knew him well. When you think no one understands your loneliness, remember that Jesus understands. He has been there and done that and invites you to share your loneliness with Him.

Perhaps your problem is not one of loss or loneliness but one of betrayal. You feel you have been a good parent, a good friend, loyal, kind, and even generous. Yet, the very people you invest the most in disappoint you. You could have taken a trip to Europe or bought a new car with the money you invested in that child/grandchild/friend and he or she doesn't really appreciate your sacrifice. In fact, they use what you give them unwisely and seem to expect even more. You feel betrayed.

Jesus had some special friends whom He hand picked and had only three years to train for ministry. These were the twelve disciples he mentored. Yet, Judas betrayed him, leading to his death, Peter denounced him, and we read in *Matthew 26:56* , **Then all the disciples deserted him and fled.** Every one of Jesus' most precious friends turned their backs on him. You think no one understands your feelings of betrayal and abandonment? Jesus has been there and done that. Jesus understands.

Do you have serious fears for the future? Perhaps you or someone you love is facing surgery or is terminally ill or you may soon have to move out of the house you lived in much of your life and you never before felt such helplessness. How do you put your feelings into words? You don't need to. Read *Luke 22:39-44.* ***Jesus went out as usual to the Mount of Olives, and his disciples followed him. On reaching the place, he said to them, "Pray that you will not fall into temptation." He withdrew about a stone's throw beyond them, knelt down and prayed, "Father, if you are willing, take this cup from me; yet not my will, but yours be done." An angel from heaven appeared to him and strengthened him. And being in anguish, he prayed more earnestly; and his sweat was like drops of blood falling to the ground.***

Unlike us, Jesus knew what the future held for him and it was so agonizing that he prayed in anguish and his sweat was like drops of blood. We all need someone to talk to, share with and confide in like a friend, family member or a good counselor. Don't leave Jesus out. Remember that He has been there and done that. He truly understands better than any earthly listener can because he endured pain far beyond anything we will experience and he wants to comfort you and me. Don't leave the earthly listener out, either. Your faith may be a powerful witness to that person.

# Universal Language

WHAT IS IT that defies all language, needs no language and is sometimes better off without language yet is often a language unto itself? The answer is *music!* A tune can be played in any part of the world and enjoyed. It may have lyrics, but they are not necessary. A Straus waltz or a John Phillip Sousa march is sufficient unto itself. It does not need words.

Hymns are an endangered species in this day of praise choruses and video projectors. Praise choruses are good and I see the value of projecting words onto a screen but I hope we can find a blend of new praise music and familiar hymns.

Let me share some words about five hymns you may recognize, all directly related to scripture. My information came from the book, *THEN SINGS MY SOUL,* giving brief accounts of the history of 300 familiar hymns. I want you to see how rich our musical heritage is and understand that these now familiar old songs did not just happen. Someone didn't whistle the tune a few times and put words to it and use it in church. Your hymnal is full of songs that came from strife, prophecy and revelation. They reflect hardship, pain and hope.

Until recently, the Dead Sea Scrolls were our oldest copies of biblical text. But in 1979, a Villanova professor and an archaeologist were excavating a site near Jerusalem. In a burial cave, they saw something that resembled the metal cap of a pencil. It was a sensational find, a tiny silver scroll of great antiquity; so small and fragile, it took years to painstakingly clean and open it. When finally unrolled, it was the world's oldest copy of a biblical text, word for word, from the book of *Numbers*: **The Lord bless you and keep you. The Lord make His face shine upon you and be gracious to you. The Lord lift up His countenance upon you and give you peace**. It was written 1,400 years before the birth of Christ. Music was added in the 1800s. The hymn is THE LORD BLESS YOU. Perhaps you recognize it as a familiar benediction.

*Matt. 28:19* **Go therefore and make disciples of all the nations, baptizing them in the name of the Father and of the Son and of the Holy Spirit**. Only one missionary is honored with a global holiday and only one is known by his own distinct color of green – St. Patrick, missionary to Ireland. He was born in AD 373 in what is now called Scotland. When he was sixteen years old, pirates raided his little town. He hid in the bushes but the pirates spotted him, captured him, and hauled him aboard a ship where he was taken to Ireland as a slave. There, he gave his life to the Lord Jesus. Eventually, he escaped and returned home to the delight of his family but, one night in a dream, he saw an Irishman pleading with him to return to and evangelize Ireland. It was a difficult decision but he did return and his life was often in danger. He became one of the greatest evangelists of all time, planting about 200 churches and baptizing 100,000 converts. In 1905, these words were set to a traditional Irish folk song called "Slane," named for an area in Ireland where Patrick reportedly challenged the local enemy with the gospel. The hymn is BE THOU MY VISION.

*Psalm 46:1* **God is our refuge and strength, a very present help in trouble**. We think of Martin Luther as a great reformer, Bible translator, political leader, fiery preacher and theologian but he was also a musician. He helped revive congregational singing and wrote a number of hymns. Some of them had borrowed tunes and they were scrapped because they sounded too much like bar and tavern music. His most famous hymn is based on Psalm 46. It reflects his intense struggle with Satan. Luther faced the power of a corrupt Roman Catholic Church and, like David and Goliath, single handedly brought the enemy to its knees and returned Christianity to biblical truth. His struggles led him to write A MIGHTY FORTRESS IS OUR GOD.

*Romans 10:13* **For whoever calls on the name of the Lord shall be saved**. Though the 1949 Los Angeles Crusade was to launch Billy Graham to world wide fame, the meetings appeared to get off to a slow start. Mr. Graham gave a news conference prior to the crusade and eagerly waited for the next day to see how the crusade would be publicized. Not a single newspaper carried the story. However, among Mr. Graham's supporters was an influential Presbyterian Bible teacher who invited Billy to her home in Beverly Hills to speak to a group of Hollywood personalities. Present that day was a hard drinking star of cowboy westerns named Stuart Hamblen who also hosted one of the most popular afternoon radio shows on the West Coast. He was known for his gambling and brawling. The two men took a liking to each other and Billy longed to win Stuart to Christ but the three week campaign neared its end and there was no sign that the big cowboy was under conviction.

The local crusade organizers sensed that the momentum for the meetings was building and suggested they extend them but Billy was hesitant. They had never done that before. He asked God for a sign. At 4:30 the next morning, his phone rang. It was Stuart Hamblen in tears. Billy woke his wife and friends and asked them to pray while Stuart and his wife drove to the hotel. That night, Stuart gave his heart to the Lord Jesus. It was the sign

Billy needed to extend the meetings.

Meanwhile, Stuart excitedly told of his conversion on his radio show and local newspapers picked up the story. Soon all of Los Angeles was buzzing about the Billy Graham meetings. The resulting publicity launched a half-century of mass evangelism virtually unparalleled in Christian history. Shortly afterward, it is reported that Stuart Hamblen met movie star John Wayne on a street and the actor asked, "What's this I hear about you, Stuart?" "Well, Duke, it's no secret what God can do," Stuart replied. "Sounds like a song," said John. Stuart went home, sat down at his piano and wrote the song, IT IS NO SECRET. He went on to write 225 other songs before his death. Whenever you sing this song, remember how discouraged Billy Graham was that not one newspaper gave his crusade a word of publicity and then the Lord worked on the heart of a hard drinking, brawling gambler who happened to have a popular radio program and with one announcement of Stuart's conversion, the World Wide Billy Graham Crusade was launched.

*Jeremiah 31:17, **There is hope in your future, says the Lord**.* When Bill & Gloria Gaither started their family in the '60s, our country was in turmoil with racial tension, the Vietnam conflict and student rebellion. They were trying to write songs with lasting answers to the turmoil of the human spirit. Then, several things happened that tested their own convictions. Gloria was pregnant sooner than they had planned to have another child. Bill got mononucleosis, leaving him exhausted and discouraged. Pondering global and personal issues, they asked each other, "What's happening to our world? If there are so many problems now, what will it be like in fifteen or twenty years? What does this child face?" Gaithers realized that courage does not come from a stable world, for the world has never been stable. We have babies, raise families, and risk living because the Resurrection is true. A few weeks after baby Benjamin was born, the song, BECAUSE HE LIVES was born in their souls and has reassured all Christians that the Lord's Resurrection is the central truth of life. Because He Lives, we can face tomorrow.

# Thanks

I WAS THE volunteer coordinator for a hospice in northern California for several years. After interviewing a patient and family, I assigned the volunteer to them that I considered most appropriate. Only once did I encounter a delicate situation. A twenty-eight year old man came to us from the Bay Area of San Francisco where he had already been trained as a volunteer. After meeting and talking with him, I knew he would be a real asset to our program, with one exception. "I'm a mortician," he replied in answer to my question about his livelihood. Since we worked with terminally ill patients, I wondered if it would appear as a conflict of interest. I wondered about the patient's acceptance.

Daily, I prayed for guidance and did not assign the volunteer immediately. Then, one day I visited a new patient who was retired and in a hospital bed in his living room. As we talked, I asked, "Mr. Johnson, when you were younger and employed, what kind of work did you do?" "I was an embalmer," he replied, and right out loud I said, "Oh, thank you, Jesus!" I finally found an appropriate assignment for the young mortician and the two men became fast friends. Mr. Johnson told the volunteer how they did things in the old days and the young man amazed Mr. Johnson with the new technology that is used today. Fortunately, they had many weeks to become acquainted and, when Mr. Johnson was nearing death, he asked the young mortician to prepare his body for burial. The young man said it would be a privilege.

Many, many times, I thanked God for answer to that prayer. I wasn't praying for world peace but for something small and simple, like placing the right volunteer with the right patient in order to give that man dignity and quality to his remaining life. God poured out His grace upon that situation; a common, everyday occurrence, ordinary stuff which I believe was made better through prayer and trust.

All of us are thankful for good things that happen but, some people are actually grateful for adversity that came through no fault of their own and totally changed their lives. Christopher Reeves, the actor who played Superman in the movies, severed his spinal cord in an accident during a horseback riding competition. He was paralyzed from the neck down and often needed assistance just to breathe. Yet, he turned that tragedy into public awareness about spinal cord injury and was instrumental in very successful fundraising for that cause. His life was suddenly altered from the hero actor to the totally paralyzed man who could not feed himself or move without assistance. He became a *powerful* voice for the handicapped. Society is thankful for people like Christopher Reeves and others who use their adversity for a higher cause.

John Walsh and his wife were an ordinary couple with a six-year-old son, Adam. One day, on a shopping trip to Sears with his mother, Adam watched some boys playing a video game while his mother shopped close by. Adam disappeared. He was kidnapped and killed. This tragedy almost ended the Walsh's marriage but they struggled to stay together and move forward with a new focus. John Walsh was determined to organize law enforcement nationally in order to identify predators and to find lost children. He was asked to host the TV program, "America's Most Wanted," and, three days after the first program aired, the criminal being sought was captured. John Walsh and his wife turned tragedy of the worst kind into action in order to prevent that same tragedy from happening to other children and their parents. John was not a celebrity like Christopher Reeves but an ordinary citizen like you and me. He and his wife thanked the thousands of people who heard of their plight and prayed for them and they went through the United States Congress to foster change in our laws; ordinary people doing extra-ordinary things as a result of adversity.

Most of us have experienced adversity and despair. We want to run away but we can't. Maybe we delay reality with alcohol or drugs, but that just compounds the problem. We need to trust God enough to believe He *will* help us and deliver us so we can cause change for the better. We may not change the world but we can make a big difference in our world - the world around us. The way we handle problems affects not just us but our family, co-workers and friends. If we come out stronger than before, then others will see that strength and want it, too. We can confidently tell them about our faith in God and our dependence on prayer.

Until John Walsh spearheaded the child protection program, there was little coordination between law enforcement agencies to help identify missing children or their abductors. There was no Amber Alert. John and his wife used the most horrendous experience in their lives to spearhead a program that has saved thousands of children from abduction and possible murder and has put predators into prison. We may not have the opportunity or privilege of serving others in a public way but, even our private and personal service to others is serving God. All service is valuable.

# Final Burp

IT WAS PREDICTED to be a hot June day. "I can't do much about the weather," I thought, "but I have to talk to son, Dave, about his hairy face." His cheeks and chin sprouted peach fuzz with a few hairs here and there. Daughter, Diane, was being married that afternoon. I cornered fifteen year old David and said, "You will be one good looking dude in that tux this afternoon." He smiled. I continued, "But, you need to do something about your face." "What's the matter with my face, Mom?" he questioned. I told him it looked dirty. No real whiskers were visible yet.

"I think you should shave," I said, and it was obvious I had paid him a very large compliment by even suggesting he shave where there were yet no whiskers. He disappeared into the bathroom and made his grand exit after a much-too-long stay. I carefully examined the face and reluctantly admitted it looked better but still left much to be desired.

The wedding was lovely. Diane looked radiant and Dave looked clean. It wasn't until two days later that we realized he had not put a blade into the razor.

# A New Spin

WE NEED TO get the word out that we are here and in the business of sharing the love of God with the community. How do they do it on television? How do they advertise products and services that we may not need and may not even *want* but we purchase them because of the advertising techniques? Are we missing a real opportunity? Why don't we try some of those successful techniques?

*Are you lonely, depressed, overweight? Is the IRS breathing down your neck? Then call the number at the bottom of your screen*

*1-800-J-E-S-U-S\**

*Call on the name of Jesus and you may find answers to some of your concerns. It will give you a peace and comfort you haven't experienced before. Do you have stomach problems, restless leg syndrome, chronic headaches? Then call the number at the bottom of your screen,*

*1-800-J-E-S-U-S.*

*It may not make these aches and pains go away but it may give you a peace and comfort that helps relieve some of your stress. Do you have financial burdens, is your marriage going down the bowl, are your children out of hand, do you hate your job? Then, call the number at the bottom of your screen,*

*1-800-J-E-S-U-S.*

*You will find a source of comfort you have never known before.*

***But wait! There's more!*** *When you call, we will send you a "How To" book like none you have ever read before. It's called the Bible. In it, you will find stories of courage and overcoming difficult obstacles. That's not all! Call within the next ten minutes and we will send you two "How To" books plus a children's book full of colorful pictures and wonderful true stories of heroes in the Bible. We're not through yet! If you live a life of guilt, of fear, if you're angry or feel misunderstood and you know you need something, it is probably forgiveness. By calling the number at the bottom of your screen,*

*1-800-J-E-S-U-S,*

***within the next ten minutes****, you are ten minutes closer to learning the truth about forgiveness of your sins and eternal life with God. How much is this wonderful offer, you ask? Well, here's the best news of all. It's FREE to you. Jesus has paid **YOUR** price. He suffered a painful and humiliating death in order for you to no longer suffer. This is an offer you just can't refuse and it's yours for the asking.*

And, if you want to know more; if you want to meet people just like you who are forgiven and want to share their lives with you, then call the number of your local Bible based church for information.

It is the second best call you will ever make.


*not a real number

# Detours

*JOB 1:1-3,* **In the land of Uz there lived a man whose name was Job. This man was blameless and upright; he feared God and shunned evil. He had seven sons and three daughters, and he owned seven thousand sheep, three thousand camels, five hundred yoke of oxen and five hundred donkeys, and had a large number of servants. He was the greatest of man among all the people of the East,** and he lost it all through no fault of his own.

Several years ago, I made a few trips to the Midwest to visit my daughter and family. I became acquainted with my granddaughters' pre-school teacher who proudly told me about her daughter, Jolynn who was an outstanding gymnast. Soon to graduate from high school, Jolynn was being considered for a scholarship by more than one university. She had won top honors over all competitors from other schools and seemed to have an innate ability for timing and grace of movement.

Although she was still a novice, coaches saw Olympic possibilities in Jolynn's future, with the proper coaching. Not just an outstanding athlete, she maintained high scholastic grades and understood that, if she truly wanted to be an Olympic quality competitor, she needed to discipline herself and sacrifice some of the social life her friends were enjoying in order to practice several hours a day. She was totally dedicated, seldom complained, and enjoyed learning new procedures, repeating them over and over until they were perfectly executed.

One day, shortly before graduation, Jolynn received two letters in the mail. The first one she opened congratulated her upon receiving a full four-year scholarship, all expenses paid, to an outstanding university. She would represent that school in national competition while being trained by some of the country's most highly regarded instructors. This was a dream come true, one she worked hard for and deserved.

The other letter was from her family doctor who had given her a routine physical recently and ordered tests because she was complaining of discomfort in her back and wondered if she had strained a muscle. The doctor, who had treated Jolynn's family for years, wrote just a few personal words. "Jolynn - the tests we took recently reveal that you are developing a degeneration in your spine due to (he named the disease). Knowing how hard you have worked toward your goal of high gymnastic achievement, I am sorry to tell you that you must cease all exercise immediately. Keeping you quiet will hopefully retard the progress of the disease which has already caused some serious spinal damage."

I wish I could tell you more about Jolynn but that was about the time my daughter's family moved from the area and I no longer went there. My guess is that, after a period of anger, fear and mourning the loss of her hopes and dreams, Jolynn recognized that she had come to a detour in life and needed to go a different direction. Her mother said they were a Christian family and I wouldn't doubt but what she went through some difficult struggles with her faith but, from what her mother told me at our last meeting, Jolynn believed that God had a plan for her. She always assumed it was in gymnastics. Now she was faced with a detour.

Most detours are hard because they shake up our control.

They force us to refocus - to think of alternatives we had not considered. We may have had to move just when we felt comfortable and established where we were. Perhaps there was an unprepared-for pregnancy or just the opposite; a yearning desire for a child that could not be fulfilled. Maybe a habit, drugs or alcohol or pornography or some kind of abuse has affected our families. You and I know that when one family member succumbs, the entire family suffers and a variety of detours occur. Some of us have had a severe financial setback or an unexpected layoff at work. Like Job, we start out confidently in one direction, thinking we know our destination when a detour suddenly occurs and totally changes everything. For a while, it may take us in a direction we do not want to go but have no choice.

It is what we do with the detour that matters. If it is unexpected and we come upon it suddenly and have to make split-second decisions, they might not be as good as those detours we see ahead that give us time to make a plan. We begin to scan the "Help Wanted" section of the paper or delay an expensive vacation because that would not be a wise financial move right now. There's a possible detour ahead.

A friend of mine worked in the food delivery industry and was invited to a corporate meeting in Chicago. Twenty-eight people in his position, from various parts of the country, received similar invitations. The reason for the meeting was not revealed but they assumed the company was introducing new products or had some other positive motive for inviting this many top employees together. When they were all assembled, the CEO stood, thanked them for being there, and announced that their jobs were being terminated. All twenty eight. The company was adopting new cost-cutting procedures and this is how they chose to announce the plan and give the twenty eight two weeks' notice.

My friend experienced a sudden, unexpected detour. He was a middle-aged man with children in college and other financial demands that loomed before him as he considered the possibility of job-hunting. Like Job, he was caught by complete surprise.

Joni Erickson was a teenager when she went swimming with friends and dove into a rock that was not visible. Instantly, she became a quadriplegic, shattering any hopes and dreams she had of a normal adult life. Prior to the accident, she excelled in art and saw that as a possible career pursuit. Now, she had to accept that it would never happen - until an art instructor told her that the skill was not in her hands but in her brain. She learned to hold a paint brush in her teeth and is well known for her religious art work. She went on to become an inspiration to others with handicaps as well as the general public.

A movie on her life showed a close-up view while she explained that, prior to her accident; she was a luke-warm Christian and, in her entire lifetime, would probably not tell more than a few people what God meant to her. "Now," she said, "I have the opportunity to share my faith with many more people." As she spoke, the camera panned back to reveal that she was alone on a stage and an audience of about 10,000 people surrounded her. By the detour she was forced to take, God had multiplied the possibilities to share her faith. *James 1:2-4:* **Consider it pure joy, my brothers, whenever you face trials of many kinds, because you know that the testing of your faith develops perseverance. Perseverance must finish its work so that you may be mature and complete, not lacking anything.**

Job and Jolynn and my cousin were not at all responsible for the detour that took them in another direction. Joni was, perhaps, a victim of poor judgment as she dove into unknown territory and instantly became a quadriplegic and was forced to take some dramatic detours.

Chuck Colson, on the other hand, purposely disobeyed rules of conduct and paid for his disobedience with a prison term. He was a bright, intelligent lawyer and special counsel to President Nixon. He became involved in the Watergate Affair, a break-in and theft of information belonging to the Democratic Party. The President resigned and several staff members went to prison. It was there that Chuck Colson saw many injustices that he felt could be corrected.

A friend introduced him to the forgiving savior, Jesus Christ, and Colson humbly sought forgiveness and direction for his future. God led him to begin a program called Prison Fellowship that helped many prisoners to accept Christ and to rely on the Holy Spirit for direction, whether they remained in prison for life or were released. Besides Bible Studies and other religious programs, Prison Fellowship offers classes to the prisoner and his/her partner and family, to adjust to their release and return home. It created a program to assure prisoners that their children will receive Christmas gifts and it trains and monitors volunteers who visit prison inmates.

This is what Colson wrote as he waited to speak in a prison: "My mind drifted back in time to scholarships and honors earned, cases argued and won, great decisions made from lofty government offices. My life had been the perfect success story - the great American dream fulfilled. All at once, I realized it was not my successes that God had used to enable me to help those in this prison or hundreds just like them. My life of success was not what made this morning so glorious. All my achievements meant nothing in God's economy. The real legacy of my life was my biggest failure. I was an ex-convict. My greatest humiliation, being sent to prison, was the beginning of God's greatest use of my life. He chose that one experience of which I could have no personal glory to provide for His kingdom all the glory!" *Hebrews 13:3,* **Remember those in prison as if you were their fellow prisoners, and those who are mistreated as if yourselves were suffering.**

Whether we have no control over the detour, like Job and Jolynn; whether we use poor judgment, as Joni Erickson may have done; or whether we intentionally disobey like Chuck Colson, God wants us to know that He can turn our detours into golden opportunities. No matter what the circumstance, no matter what the sin, Jesus has already paid the price. We don't need to wallow in self pity or the depression of regret. Detours happen. It's how we accept them and allow God to use us as a result of them that counts.

# Love's Full Circle

OUR PHONE RARELY rang after nine pm so, when the call came in at 10:30, I braced myself for bad news. It was quite the opposite. My daughter Diane's voice was at such a high pitch, I had to ask her to slow down and start over. "Mom," she cried, "you'll never guess who just called from Kentucky." She didn't wait for a reply. "Barbara! Foster daughter, Barbara!" I flattened my hand to my heart and sat down before my knees had a chance to buckle.

Time evaporated as I flashed back to a warm summer day in 1957 and watched a social worker pull her car into our driveway. Out of it emerged our first two foster children, a scrawny seven year old Barbara and her nine year old half brother, Richard. They each carried a paper shopping bag that held their clothes and any worldly possessions. Our own daughter, 2 ½ year old Diane, had a closet and dresser full while these two young visitors would only need a couple of hangers and half a drawer to accommodate their wardrobes.

Days melted into weeks that melted into months as Richard and Barbara continued to make our family more complete. After six months into their stay, the fateful call came from the social worker that the children would be moving. Their mother was relocating to a larger city and wanted them near her. We offered to drive them there every weekend if she allowed them to remain with us but she refused. The children's teachers even appealed to our governor because they saw such a remarkable improvement as the result of living in a stable home but the governor would not hear the case.

As they piled boxes and bags into the car, and then found room to squeeze themselves in, I fought back the urge to scream, "Don't go. Please," but they disappeared down the road and I could only hope that some day we would be reunited. The policy of the Agency was that foster families not attempt to contact children after they left the home.

I had no idea that losing them would hurt so much. I grieved to the depth of my soul but never lost hope that we might meet again and I prayed for them regularly. Over the years, twelve more foster children shared our home and I did my best to mother them in such a way that they could take good, solid, memories along when they left. As technology improved and the computer became a valuable resource, I tried to search for both Richard and Barbara, to no avail. Then, almost fifty years later, came the very special phone call.

By the time Diane reached me, it was close to midnight in Kentucky but she encouraged me to call anyway. "She's waiting, Mom," so I excitedly dialed the number and two souls, separated for half a century, reconnected. Barbara told me how she tried for years to contact me through a variety of organizations and resources, to no avail. No wonder since, twenty years after the children left us, I became divorced, moved, eventually remarried and changed my name. Yet, she persisted despite a variety of setbacks. We talked until the wee hours of the morning.

Barbara had not lost her gift for gab. She told me about the places she had called "home" after leaving us, about working her way through college in Oregon where she met her husband, Lanny, about her seven children, all born at home and home schooled. The two oldest girls were married now with children of their own. Imagine! My little foster girl, a grandmother. She shared that, although she and Richard were separated as children, they later reunited and still keep in touch. Their mother died a few years ago.

I knew nothing about Kentucky except the stereotype misconceptions seen on TV, dusty back roads leading to a still. When I asked Barbara what her family did for enjoyment, she replied, "Well, actually, we sing acappella classical music. Would you like a CD?" Kentucky took on a vibrant new identity after that.

Barbara and I accepted the probability that we would not meet again since my home in Idaho was a long distance from hers but we corresponded regularly via email and made occasional phone calls. During the next couple of years, my husband became ill with cancer and died. Then, I contracted cancer and had successful surgery to remove it. Through all this, Barbara emailed encouragement and telephoned often. It was one of those calls that changed everything and gave hope to a possible reunion.

In February of 2007 Barbara called and said, "My oldest son is being married in Boise in June. Will you come?" I was touched and honored and told her I would be there. Boise was 400 miles from my home. I told Barbara that I lived near Yellowstone National Park in one direction and the Teton Mountains in another, both very popular tourist attractions. Her next call brought me to my feet with excitement. "My husband and I want to take our three youngest children, all teenagers, on a sight-seeing tour, since we are driving cross country, and would like to include the places you mentioned." I immediately invited them to stay with me and use my home as a base for their itinerary and they accepted.

Once again, I anxiously waited for a car to arrive that would carry a girl who touched my life so deeply many years ago and

I wondered how she would look now. When she stepped out of the car, I knew I would have recognized her in a crowd. Fifty years had not erased the memories and, when her eyes met mine, they were eyes of a little girl I could never forget. I bonded quickly with the family and the children called me Grandma. They fished off the riverbank behind my home and baked bread for me. They listened to stories about Barbara when she was young. Then, they headed for Boise and I followed later.

It was a beautiful, warm day for the wedding. The entire Thompson family gathered outside for pictures and I watched from a distance. When it was time for one grand family photo, someone asked the photographer to wait while they called me over to join them. I could hardly believe it. They wanted *me* in the family picture.

We made our way into the church for the ceremony and the family took their place in the front two rows while I watched comfortably from the back pew. It happened again. Just before the ceremony began, Lanny walked back to where I was sitting and invited me to join the family in front. The circle was complete. Fifty years earlier, I invited Barbara to join our family and now she and her family returned the invitation. It was the "story book ending," not to a fairy tale but to a real life experience. In my own limited humanness, I could never have imagined such a joyous reunion.

The most profound lesson I learned from this entire experience is that we influence certain others, and they influence us through this journey we call *life*, even though our paths cross for but a short time. By just being ourselves, displaying no unusual talent, we so strongly affect each other that we make some special effort to reunite. Sometimes we search. Sometimes we almost frantically hunt. And, if we are very, very lucky, we find.

# Out-of-Body

ONE LAST STORY needs to be shared. I have not told this to many people because it is weird, but it is true and it happened to me. Early in the 1990s, my vision took a nose dive and I hesitated driving, especially in the rain at night. Street lights became bursting fireworks in the sky and reading was impossible without a magnifying glass. It was time to have my first cataract removed. My visit to an ophthalmologist left me in doubt because he was so young. I inquired about his age and he said that he was twenty-eight and, if I preferred someone older, he would arrange for that. I felt foolish and did not want to embarrass him. I also rationalized in my mind that being so young put him into the bracket of, "most up-to-date in training and equipment." He would be my surgeon. I often wondered, but never asked, if I was his first patient.

On the day of surgery, my husband gave me one last good-bye kiss and I disappeared thought the swinging doors from the waiting room to the unknown. A nurse advised me to lay down on a gurney. The surgeon arrived and introduced me to an older doctor who was an anesthesiologist. It surprised me to have another specialist there when this was supposed to be such a simple, "easy-in easy-out" procedure. Now, I became more certain that this was the young man's first surgery in that hospital and the extra physician was there for quality control and assistance.

I took a couple of pills the ophthalmologist-surgeon said would make me relax. The painless procedure did not require me to be unconscious. Then the surgeon pulled my lower eyelid down with one hand and inserted a long needle, from what appeared to be a large syringe, deeply into my lower lid. I have a high tolerance for pain but this was the most painful procedure I ever experienced. I told myself to restrain from any startling noise. I reminded myself that I was a strong Swede and the pain would soon leave. I learned later that the doctor had hit a nerve block to the brain. Then, something happened that I have a difficult time explaining because it is surreal. Nurses attending me said it was an out-of-body experience.

A very clear picture appeared in my mind. I was walking on a dirt road. For some reason, I likened it to the road to Emmaus from the Bible. Two men were walking in the same direction as me and then a third man joined them. I wondered if they were the men in the Emmaus story and if the third was the risen Christ? Their clothes were like Middle East garb and their faces were not visible to me. We walked together for some time and talked and laughed a lot. I cannot overemphasize how joyous we were.

There was a peace in this experience that I have never felt before or after it happened. Then, suddenly, a voice told me that I needed to turn around immediately. I hesitated because I did not want to hurt the other walkers' feelings. Now the voice was stronger and louder and more demanding. It said that I MUST turn around IMMEDIATELY *or it would be too late.* Apparently, I obeyed this command because I was once again on the gurney. I had jumped from lying on my back to lying on my side. Still, my mind was not yet in sync with my body because something told me that I could not bring back, with me, the peace I felt in that other experience.

It is true. I do not remember that peace but I do remember having had it and there are no words in our limited language that describe it. I can say, without any doubt, that I will never fear death. Was I in the "valley of the shadow?" I have no idea. I only believe that God allowed me a glimpse of what is to come and it so far surpasses the joy and peace that we experience here on earth, there is really no comparison.

The anesthesiologist asked me if I had ever had a seizure and I told him I had not. I asked if what I just experienced was a seizure and he said he did not know. "Your pulse stopped and your heartbeat flat-lined on the monitor for a number of seconds," he said. I asked how he revived me. "I jutted out your jaw," he replied. That was common procedure for CPR when I took the training. If that didn't work, then we went to chest compressions.

If you are seeking guidance that leaves no doubt about wanting God, and only God, to direct your life; if you honestly believe that Jesus did live and did die and did rise from the dead and considers you so valuable, He was willing to suffer, suffer, suffer and die for *you*; if you want this God, this Jesus, to live in you as the Holy Spirit, then tell Him now. Sometimes, religious rules and regulations and ritual keep God at a distance from us but don't let that happen. Go right to the Word. Invite Him into your life. ***Turn around.*** I did.

CPSIA information can be obtained at www.ICGtesting.com
Printed in the USA
BVOW071628210413

318660BV00001B/23/P